T0184204

Introduction to Linguistic Annotation and Text Analytics

Synthesis Lectures on Human Language Technologies

Editor
Graeme Hirst, *University of Toronto*

Synthesis Lectures on Human Language Technologies publishes monographs on topics relating to natural language processing, computational linguistics, information retrieval, and spoken language understanding. Emphasis is placed on important new techniques, on new applications, and on topics that combine two or more HLT subfields.

Introduction to Linguistic Annotation and Text Analytics
Graham Wilcock
2009

Dependency Parsing
Sandra Kübler, Ryan McDonald, Joakim Nivre
2009

Statistical Language Models for Information Retrieval
ChengXiang Zhai
2008

Introduction to Linguistic Annotation and Text Analytics
Graham Wilcock

ISBN: 978-3-031-01004-0   paperback
ISBN: 978-3-031-02132-9   ebook

DOI 10.1007/978-3-031-02132-9

A Publication in the Springer series
SYNTHESIS LECTURES ON ADVANCES IN AUTOMOTIVE TECHNOLOGY

Lecture #3
Series Editor: Graeme Hirst, *University of Toronto*

Series ISSN
Synthesis Lectures on Human Language Technologies
Print 1947-4040   Electronic 1947-4059

Introduction to Linguistic Annotation and Text Analytics

Graham Wilcock
University of Helsinki

SYNTHESIS LECTURES ON HUMAN LANGUAGE TECHNOLOGIES #3

ABSTRACT

Linguistic annotation and text analytics are active areas of research and development, with academic conferences and industry events such as the Linguistic Annotation Workshops and the annual Text Analytics Summits. This book provides a basic introduction to both fields, and aims to show that good linguistic annotations are the essential foundation for good text analytics.

After briefly reviewing the basics of XML, with practical exercises illustrating in-line and stand-off annotations, a chapter is devoted to explaining the different levels of linguistic annotations. The reader is encouraged to create example annotations using the WordFreak linguistic annotation tool. The next chapter shows how annotations can be created automatically using statistical NLP tools, and compares two sets of tools, the OpenNLP and Stanford NLP tools.

The second half of the book describes different annotation formats and gives practical examples of how to interchange annotations between different formats using XSLT transformations. The two main text analytics architectures, GATE and UIMA, are then described and compared, with practical exercises showing how to configure and customize them. The final chapter is an introduction to text analytics, describing the main applications and functions including named entity recognition, coreference resolution and information extraction, with practical examples using both open source and commercial tools.

Copies of the example files, scripts, and stylesheets used in the book are available from the companion website, located at `http://sites.morganclaypool.com/wilcock`.

KEYWORDS

linguistic annotation, statistical natural language processing, part-of-speech tagging, named entity recognition, information extractions, text analytics

Contents

Preface

Today, human language technologies are not only academic research topics, but also fields for commercial applications. That is particularly true of the subjects addressed in this book.

On the academic side, *linguistic annotation* is currently an active research area. The Linguistic Annotation Workshop (Boguraev et al. 2007) at the 2007 conference of the Association for Computational Linguistics was very successful and led to the founding of SIGANN, a Special Interest Group for Annotation. On the commercial side, *text analytics* is the name given to an emerging field of information technology. There are now regular industry events such as the annual Text Analytics Summit (http://www.textanalyticsnews.com), and it is claimed that "text technologies …have entered the business mainstream" (Grimes 2008).

WHO THE BOOK IS FOR

The book is intended to provide a basic introduction to linguistic annotation and text analytics. While we hope that even the expert reader will find material of interest, we assume very little prior knowledge.

You might be a commercial developer who urgently needs to get started on applications that will extract information from texts. If so, you may think that you need to know how to *analyze* texts, rather than how to *annotate* texts. In fact, you would be happy if you could do the analysis without doing any annotations. You want to use existing tools immediately, to find out what is possible. This book will certainly help you get started quickly with existing tools, and hopefully it will also show you that doing good annotations is the best way to do good analysis.

You might be a student with a background in computer science, who feels at home with XML and Java but uncomfortable with intransitive verbs and prepositional phrases. If so, I hope the brief explanations of linguistic terminology in Chapter 2 will be helpful. There is plenty of scope for your computing skills in text analytics, where you can use machine learning algorithms to exploit the high-quality linguistic annotations that professional linguists have provided in annotated corpora. Creative new applications are waiting to be invented.

On the other hand, you might be a researcher with a background in languages and literary studies, eager to investigate discourse phenomena, rhetorical structure or diachronic variation, or all kinds of fascinating things. You will find the basic techniques you need in this book, illustrated with standard applications such as part-of-speech tagging and syntactic parsing. If you are creative you can work out how to apply the techniques to your own area. As a reward there will be good opportunities for publishing your results.

DOING THE PRACTICAL WORK

Throughout the book there are short practical exercises that you need to do in order to acquire essential skills. This practical work uses a number of software tools that are freely available on the web. If you are working on your own, you need to know how to download and install these tools on your system.

The tools are written in Java, so you need to have Java installed before you start. The Java Runtime Environment (JRE) is sufficient, but if you are a Java programmer you can use the JDK to develop your own applications using the tool APIs. If you are not a Java programmer, you can do all the practical work in this book by running the tools as shown in the practical work examples.

For the practical exercises we provide example scripts for running XML tools and annotation tools from the Linux shell. Of course, the Linux scripts can easily be turned into equivalent Windows .bat files. The reader should check the book's website at `http://sites.morganclaypool.com/wilcock` for updates to the scripts and other resources.

ACKNOWLEDGEMENTS

The whole field of linguistic annotation is indebted to Nancy Ide for her vision and leadership for more than ten years. I am grateful to her for the opportunity of collaborating on the NLPXML series of workshops.

Chapter 1 is dedicated to Doug Tidwell, who inspired my enthusiasm for XML and XSLT over ten years ago. His brilliant IBM tutorials used Sonnet 130 as an example text, which I have used throughout Chapters 1 to 5.

Chapters 2 and 3 are dedicated to Tom Morton, in gratitude for WordFreak and OpenNLP. We are massively indebted to the many open source software developers who have given us the excellent tools used in this book, including Xerces, Xalan, jEdit, GATE, and UIMA.

Finally, as always I thank my wife Kristiina Jokinen for her support and encouragement. Like everything else that I manage to do, it was her idea that led to me writing this book.

Graham Wilcock
University of Helsinki
April 2009

CHAPTER 1

Working with XML

1.1 INTRODUCTION

The aim of this book is to help you to gain knowledge and expertise in techniques for linguistic annotation and text analytics. You will gain practical experience by using selected tools to annotate and analyze texts.

A great deal of the book is about how to create annotations, and we should be clear from the outset why this is worthwhile. The purpose of the annotations is to support subsequent applications, which produce some kind of useful results by analyzing the texts. Many of the annotations are linguistic in nature, and at first sight their relevance to the required analysis may not be obvious. Nevertheless, it often turns out that the analysis is tricky, and the only way to get the right results is to exploit the information in the linguistic annotations.

Whatever the application, when the information in the annotations is used, the ancient principle of GIGO ("garbage in, garbage out") applies: incorrect annotations inevitably lead to unsuccessful applications. To make the same point more positively:

- *Good annotations support good applications*

LINGUISTIC ANNOTATION

In general, annotations are notes of some kind that are attached to an object of some kind. In this book, the objects that are annotated are texts. Linguistic annotations are notes about linguistic features of the annotated text that give information about the words and sentences of the text. Chapters 2 and 3 show how linguistic annotations can be created by annotation tools. For example, a part-of-speech tagger adds an annotation to a word in the text to say that the word is a noun, or a verb, or some other part of speech.

The value of linguistic annotations is that they can be used by subsequent applications. For example, a text-to-speech application reads a given text out aloud using a speech synthesizer. If the word *contract* occurs in the text it can be pronounced in two different ways, as in *The economy will contract next year* or in *They will read the contract tomorrow*. In the first example *contract* is a verb, and in the second it is a noun. This is not an isolated example. Compare *read* in the second example with *They read the contract yesterday*. In both cases *read* is a verb, but the speech synthesizer must pronounce it differently when it is past tense. If a part-of-speech tagger has already added these annotations, the text-to-speech application can use them. Otherwise, the text-to-speech component has to do the part-of-speech tagging in addition to its own tasks.

TEXT ANALYTICS

Text analytics applications extract some kind of useful information from texts. For example, a named entity recognizer picks out specific types of entities that are mentioned in the text, such as companies, people, job titles and URLs. A recent commercial example is the Clearforest Calais text analytics web service (see Chapter 6, Section 6.7). The Clearforest Gnosis web browser plugin uses the Calais web service to perform named entity recognition for the web page you are viewing. Chapters 3 and 5 of this book will show you how to perform named entity recognition yourself using freely available open source tools, and how to customize text analytics applications for different types of texts.

The value of linguistic annotations is seen again in text analytics applications such as named entity recognition. The word *general* can be a job title as in *the highest-ranking general*, but in *the general opinion* it is not a job title. In the first example *general* is a noun, and in the second it is an adjective. If a part-of-speech tagger has already added these annotations, the named entity recognizer can use them to improve its precision, as shown in Chapter 6.

STRUCTURE OF THE BOOK

The book is organized as follows. Chapter 1 reviews the basics of XML and clarifies the difference between in-line and stand-off annotations. Chapter 2 describes the different levels of linguistic annotation, and encourages you to gain experience of making annotation decisions using a linguistic annotation tool, WordFreak. Chapter 3 shows how to do automatic annotations using statistical NLP tools, and compares the OpenNLP and Stanford NLP tools. Chapter 4 gives practical examples of interchanging annotations between different formats using XSLT transformations. Chapter 5 describes two architectures for text analytics, GATE and UIMA, and shows how to configure and customize them. Chapter 6 presents examples of text analytics techniques using both open source and commercial tools.

1.2   XML BASICS

This chapter reviews XML basics: editing XML, parsing and validating XML, and transforming XML. We also clarify the difference between in-line and stand-off annotations, and see why stand-off annotations are one of the recommendations of the XML Corpus Encoding Standard.

If you're unfamiliar with XML, you might want to study an introductory tutorial on the web such as Doug Tidwell's *Introduction to XML* (Tidwell 2002). There are also many books on XML: some suggestions for further study are listed in Section 1.8. However, the basics of XML can be quickly reviewed by means of a simple example.

Figure 1.1 shows Shakespeare's Sonnet 130 with XML markup. In addition to the lines of the sonnet, the file contains some basic information about the author. The first line, `<?xml version="1.0"?>`, is an *XML header* which confirms that the file is XML. Yes, XML is still on version 1.0.

Every XML document must have exactly one *root element*. Here, the root element is the sonnet element, which starts on the second line with the `<sonnet>` tag, and ends on the last line with the `</sonnet>` tag. The sonnet element has an *attribute*. The attribute's name is type and its value is *Shakespearean*.

The sonnet element has three *child elements*: author, title and lines. The author element in turn has five child elements. The title element has no child elements, but it has *text content*. Its text content is *Sonnet 130*. The lines element has 14 child elements, each of which is a line element. Each line element holds one line of the sonnet as its text content.

EDITING XML

You can edit XML with any text editor. In the practical work sections, we'll use jEdit (`http://www.jedit.org`) to edit XML files. Like most of the tools in this book, jEdit is free, open source, Java-based, and platform-independent.

Another reason for using jEdit is that it has a wide range of easy-to-install plugins which provide convenient support for most XML processing tasks. Some of jEdit's capabilities as an advanced XML editor are described by LePage and Wellens (2003). We'll use jEdit XML plugin to do XML parsing and validation (see Section 1.3) and we'll use jEdit XSLT plugin to do XML transformations (see Section 1.4).

```
<?xml version="1.0"?>
<sonnet type="Shakespearean">
  <author>
    <last-name>Shakespeare</last-name>
    <first-name>William</first-name>
    <nationality>British</nationality>
    <year-of-birth>1564</year-of-birth>
    <year-of-death>1616</year-of-death>
  </author>
  <title>Sonnet 130</title>
  <lines>
    <line>My mistress' eyes are nothing like the sun,</line>
    <line>Coral is far more red than her lips red.</line>
    <line>If snow be white, why then her breasts are dun,</line>
    <line>If hairs be wires, black wires grow on her head.</line>
    <line>I have seen roses damasked, red and white,</line>
    <line>But no such roses see I in her cheeks.</line>
    <line>And in some perfumes is there more delight</line>
    <line>Than in the breath that from my mistress reeks.</line>
    <line>I love to hear her speak, yet well I know</line>
    <line>That music hath a far more pleasing sound.</line>
    <line>I grant I never saw a goddess go,</line>
    <line>My mistress when she walks, treads on the ground.</line>
    <line>And yet, by Heaven, I think my love as rare</line>
    <line>As any she belied with false compare.</line>
  </lines>
</sonnet>
```

Figure 1.1: sonnet130.xml. Sonnet 130 with XML markup (Tidwell 2000).

Figure 1.2 shows sonnet130.xml being edited in jEdit. The structure of the XML document is shown in the Sidekick panel on the right.

1.3   XML PARSING AND VALIDATION

There are many XML parsers, including many that are free, open source and easy to download. The one we will use is the Apache Software Foundation's Xerces-Java XML parser (http://xerces.apache.org/xerces2-j/). We'll use Xerces to parse and validate XML files. The Xerces parser can be used from the command line or it can be run inside jEdit using jEdit XML plugin.

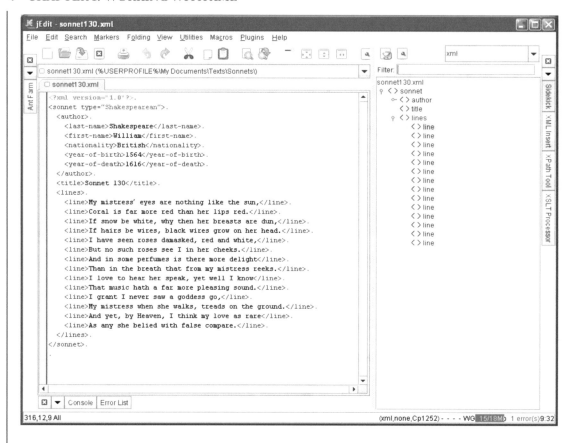

Figure 1.2: Editing `sonnet130.xml` with jEdit XML plugin.

PRACTICAL WORK: PARSING XML FROM THE COMMAND LINE

1. The shell script shown in Figure 1.3 runs the Xerces Java XML parser. Change the value of XERCES_HOME to the name of the directory where you installed Xerces. Make the script executable (`chmod +x xerces.sh`). The script takes input from a file.

2. Use it like this to parse `sonnet130.xml`:
   `./xerces.sh sonnet130.xml &`.

PRACTICAL WORK: INSTALLING JEDIT XML PLUGIN

1. Start jEdit and open Plugin Manager from the Plugins menu. In Plugin Manager, select the Install tab. In the Install tab, tick SideKick, XercesPlugin and XML. Click the Install button to install them.

2. Use jEdit's menus to open SideKick, XMLInsert and ErrorList. Using the docking options, dock SideKick and XMLInsert on the right, and ErrorList at the bottom.

```
#!/bin/sh
# xerces.sh. A script to run Xerces Java XML parser
# G. Wilcock 21.11.2007
#
# Usage: xerces.sh [-options] filename.xml
#
# Parse without validation:  xerces.sh filename.xml
# Validation with DTD:       xerces.sh -v filename.xml
# Validation with Schema:    xerces.sh -v -s filename.xml


XERCES_HOME=~gwilcock/Tools/xerces-2_9_1


CLASSPATH=.:\
$XERCES_HOME/xercesImpl.jar:\
$XERCES_HOME/xercesSamples.jar:\
$XERCES_HOME/xml-apis.jar
export CLASSPATH


java sax.Counter $*
```

Figure 1.3: `xerces.sh`. A script to run Xerces Java XML parser.

PRACTICAL WORK: PARSING XML IN JEDIT

1. Open `sonnet130.xml`, the XML version of Sonnet 130, in jEdit. Use SideKick to view the document structure. Use SideKick's Parse button to check that it is syntactically well-formed.

2. Deliberate mistake 1: Edit `sonnet130.xml` by changing the first `<line>` start tag to `<ligne>`. Parse it again. It is now syntactically ill-formed. There is an error message in the Error List panel as shown in Figure 1.4.

3. Deliberate mistake 2: Edit the file further by changing the first `</line>` end tag to `</ligne>`. Parse it again. Is it now well-formed or ill-formed? It should be syntactically well-formed, because the incorrect start tag `<ligne>` is correctly matched by the incorrect end tag `</ligne>`.

XML VALIDATION

XML is validated using Document Type Definitions (DTDs) or XML Schemas. Further details on DTDs and Schemas can be found from the references in Section 1.8. Here we show a simple example of validation with a DTD.

Figure 1.5 shows a DTD for sonnets, from (Tidwell 2004). It's called a Document Type Definition because it defines a particular type of document. It shows which elements are permitted in documents of the defined type, and how the elements are nested in the permitted document structure.

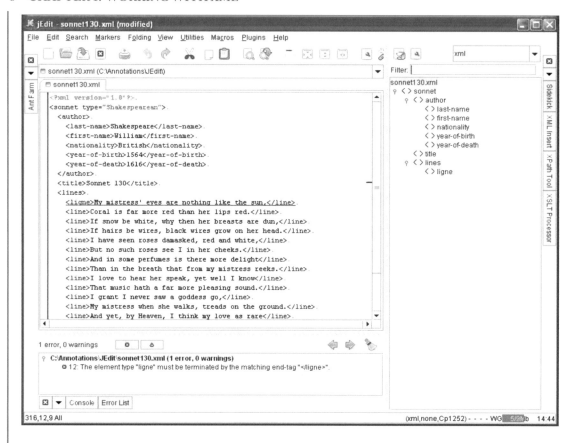

Figure 1.4: Parsing `sonnet130.xml` with jEdit XML plugin.

This DTD says that the `<author>`, `<title>` and `<lines>` elements are nested inside the `<sonnet>` element in that order, but `<title>` may be omitted. The `<sonnet>` element has an attribute list (ATTLIST) with one attribute named type, whose value can be either Shakespearean or Petrarchan, with a default of Shakespearean.

The `<author>` element contains at least `<last-name>`, `<first-name>` and `<nationality>` elements, optionally followed by either `<year-of-birth>` or `<year-of-death>` or both. These five elements are text strings (#PCDATA). The `<lines>` element contains 14 `<line>` elements, which are strings.

PRACTICAL WORK: VALIDATING XML IN JEDIT
In the parsing example, we checked only for well-formedness. Now we see how validation goes beyond this. For this part, you need to have `sonnet.dtd` in the same folder/directory as `sonnet130.xml`.

1. Open `sonnet130.xml` in jEdit and insert the line

```
<!-- The root element is sonnet -->
<!ELEMENT sonnet  (author,title?,lines)>
<!-- The default sonnet type is "Shakespearean" -->
<!ATTLIST sonnet  type (Shakespearean | Petrarchan)
                       "Shakespearean">


<!-- author contains information about the author -->
<!ELEMENT author  (last-name,first-name,nationality,
                   year-of-birth?,year-of-death?)>


<!-- The elements inside author contain text -->
<!ELEMENT last-name (#PCDATA)>
<!ELEMENT first-name (#PCDATA)>
<!ELEMENT nationality (#PCDATA)>
<!ELEMENT year-of-birth (#PCDATA)>
<!ELEMENT year-of-death (#PCDATA)>


<!-- The title of the sonnet -->
<!ELEMENT title (#PCDATA)>


<!-- The lines element contains exactly 14 lines -->
<!ELEMENT lines (line,line,line,line,
                 line,line,line,line,
                 line,line,line,line,
                 line,line)>


<!-- Each line element contains text -->
<!ELEMENT line (#PCDATA)>
```

Figure 1.5: sonnet.dtd. A DTD for sonnets from (Tidwell 2004).


```
<!DOCTYPE sonnet SYSTEM "sonnet.dtd">
```

immediately after the XML header. Validate the file against the DTD by clicking the Parse button. It should be well-formed and valid.

2. Deliberate mistake 1: Edit sonnet130.xml in jEdit by changing the first <line> start tag to <ligne>. Validate it again. It should now be syntactically ill-formed.

3. Deliberate mistake 2: Edit the file further by changing the first </line> end tag to </ligne>. Validate it again. Is it now valid or invalid?

4. See Figure 1.6. It is syntactically well-formed, because the start tag `<ligne>` is correctly matched by the end tag `</ligne>`, but it is invalid because the DTD does not allow `<ligne>` elements.

PRACTICAL WORK: VALIDATING XML FROM THE COMMAND LINE

1. The `xerces.sh` script in Figure 1.3 can also be used for validating XML with the Xerces parser from the command line.

2. To validate with a DTD, use the option `-v`. To validate with an XML Schema, use the two options `-v -s`.

3. Use it like this to validate `sonnet130.xml` with `sonnet.dtd`:
   `./xerces.sh -v sonnet130.xml &`.

4. Repeat the deliberate mistakes 1 and 2 above, validating the sonnet from the command line at each stage.

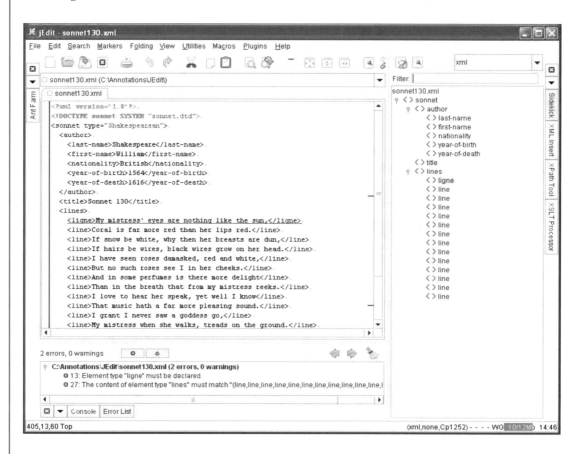

Figure 1.6: Validating `sonnet130.xml` with jEdit XML plugin.

1.4   XML TRANSFORMATIONS

One thing we will sometimes need to do is to transform XML annotations from one format to another. There are many ways to process XML files using your favourite programming or scripting language. The one we will use is the W3C standard (`http://www.w3.org/TR/xslt`): XSL Transformations (XSLT).

If you are already familiar with XSLT, you can see examples of advanced transformations between specific annotation formats in Chapter 4. Here, we present an introductory example: a simple XSLT stylesheet to transform the sonnet from XML to HTML for viewing in a web browser.

You can learn the full details about XSLT from the W3C specifications or from a textbook such as Doug Tidwell's excellent introduction (Tidwell 2001). The basic idea is that an XSLT processor reads XML input and applies transformations as specified in an XSLT stylesheet in order to produce an output. The output format can be XML, HTML or plain text - this is also specified by the stylesheet.

We'll use the Apache Software Foundation's open source Xalan-Java XSLT transformation processor (`http://xalan.apache.org/xalan-j/`). Xalan can be used from the command line or inside jEdit with jEdit XSLT plugin.

As an example, we'll use the XSLT stylesheet shown in Figures 1.9 to 1.11. This stylesheet transforms the XML version of Sonnet 130 into HTML, putting it into a table format and showing the rhyme scheme explicitly. It also colour-codes the lines of the sonnet according to the rhyme scheme, as shown in Figure 1.7. We'll do the transformation first, and look at the stylesheet details afterwards.

PRACTICAL WORK: TRANSFORMING XML FROM THE COMMAND LINE

1. The shell script shown in Figure 1.8 runs the Xalan Java XSLT processor. Change the value of XALAN_HOME to the name of the directory where you installed Xalan. Make the script executable (`chmod +x xalan.sh`).

2. Use it like this to transform Sonnet 130:
   `./xalan.sh -in sonnet130.xml -xsl sonnet-html.xsl`
   `-out sonnet130.html &`.

3. The result is `sonnet130.html`. View it in a web browser (Figure 1.7).

HOW THE STYLESHEET WORKS

The first part of the stylesheet, shown in Figure 1.9, creates the main structure of the output HTML page, with `<head>` and `<body>` elements between the `<html>` start tag and the `</html>` end tag. The `<head>` element contains a `<title>` element for the title of the web page, and the `<body>` element contains an HTML `<h3>` heading for the title of the sonnet. Both kinds of title are filled with the same value: the actual title of the sonnet, obtained from the input XML file by `<xsl:value-of select="title">`.

The `<body>` also contains a paragraph `<p>` giving various details about the author. These details are obtained from the input XML file by `<xsl:value-of>` statements, which select the required items by means of XPath expressions such as `select="author/first-name"` and `select="author/year-of-death"`. These details are formatted as desired in the output with parentheses, spaces and punctuation between `<xsl:text>` start tags and `</xsl:text>` end tags.

In the last part of the `<body>` element, the stylesheet creates an HTML `<table>` element. The rows and columns of the table will be filled in by applying further templates. This is initiated by the `<xsl:apply-templates>` statement between the `<table>` start tag and the `</table>` end tag.

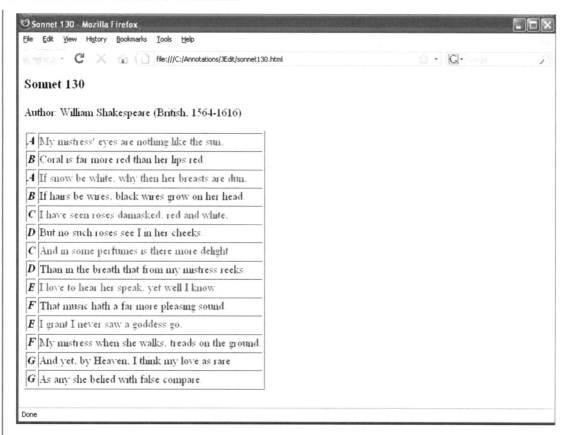

Figure 1.7: The transformed sonnet viewed in a web browser.

The remaining templates in Figures 1.10 and 1.11 specify the exact formatting of the rows and columns of the HTML table. The rows are created by `<tr>` elements, and the columns by `<td>` elements. In each row, the first column specifies the rhyme scheme by a bold, italic capital letter. The second column contains the line of the sonnet, colour-coded according to the rhyme scheme.

PRACTICAL WORK: INSTALLING JEDIT XSLT PLUGIN

1. Start jEdit and open Plugin Manager from the Plugins menu. In the Plugin Manager window, select the Install tab. In the Install tab, tick XSLT, then click the Install button to install it.

2. The XSLT plugin includes XPath Tool and XSLT Processor. Use jEdit's menus to open XSLT Processor and use the docking options to dock it at the right.

```
#!/bin/sh
# xalan.sh. A script to run Xalan Java XSLT transformer
# G. Wilcock 21.11.2007
#
# Usage: xalan.sh -in XMLfile -xsl XSLTstylesheet -out outputfile
#
# Examples:
# XML to HTML:   xalan.sh -in file.xml -xsl xml2html.xsl -out file.html
# XML to XSL-FO: xalan.sh -in file.xml -xsl xml2fo.xsl -out file.fo
# XML to SVG:    xalan.sh -in file.xml -xsl xml2svg.xsl -out file.svg

XALAN_HOME=~gwilcock/Tools/xalan-2_7_1

CLASSPATH=.:\
$XALAN_HOME/xercesImpl.jar:\
$XALAN_HOME/xml-apis.jar:\
$XALAN_HOME/xalan.jar
export CLASSPATH

java org.apache.xalan.xslt.Process $*
```

Figure 1.8: `xalan.sh`. A script to run Xalan Java XSLT processor.

PRACTICAL WORK: TRANSFORMING XML IN JEDIT

1. In jEdit XSLT panel, select `sonnet-html.xsl` as the stylesheet and select `sonnet130.xml` as the source file, or select Current Buffer if the file is currently open, as in Figure 1.12.

2. Do the transformation by clicking the "XML + XSL =" button.

3. The result, `sonnet130.html`, is shown in Figure 1.7.

1.5   IN-LINE ANNOTATIONS

When XML annotations are inserted into the text, this is called *in-line* markup. The text and annotations are mixed together in the same file. This is fine for simple annotations, but it can lead to difficulties when different types of markup are applied to the same text. The markup elements may overlap in ways that cannot be fitted into the requirements for well-formed XML syntax. We will see an example of this difficulty in the following practical work.

PRACTICAL WORK: MULTIPLE MARKUPS

1. Edit `sonnet130.xml` in jEdit. The file already has XML markup for the author details and for the layout of the lines. Add new annotations for sentence boundaries, by marking the start of each

```
<?xml version="1.0"?>
<xsl:stylesheet version="1.0"
                xmlns:xsl="http://www.w3.org/1999/XSL/Transform">

<xsl:template match="/">
  <xsl:apply-templates select="sonnet"/>
</xsl:template>

<xsl:template match="sonnet">
  <html>
    <head>
      <title><xsl:value-of select="title"/></title>
    </head>
    <body>
      <h3><xsl:value-of select="title"/></h3>
      <p>
        <xsl:text>Author: </xsl:text>
        <xsl:value-of select="author/first-name"/>
        <xsl:text> </xsl:text>
        <xsl:value-of select="author/last-name"/>
        <xsl:text> (</xsl:text>
        <xsl:value-of select="author/nationality"/>
        <xsl:text>, </xsl:text>
        <xsl:value-of select="author/year-of-birth"/>
        <xsl:text>-</xsl:text>
        <xsl:value-of select="author/year-of-death"/>
        <xsl:text>) </xsl:text>
      </p>
      <table border="1" colspec="30 *">
        <xsl:apply-templates select="//line"/>
      </table>
    </body>
  </html>
</xsl:template>
```

Figure 1.9: `sonnet-html.xsl` (Part 1): An XSLT stylesheet to transform the sonnet from XML to HTML, from (Tidwell 2000).

```
<xsl:template match="line[1]|line[3]">
  <tr>
    <td align="right"><b><i>A </i></b></td>
    <td><font color="green"><xsl:value-of select="."/></font></td>
  </tr>
</xsl:template>

<xsl:template match="line[2]|line[4]">
  <tr>
    <td align="right"><b><i> B</i></b></td>
    <td><font color="purple"><xsl:value-of select="."/></font></td>
  </tr>
</xsl:template>

<xsl:template match="line[5]|line[7]">
  <tr>
    <td align="right"><b><i>C </i></b></td>
    <td><font color="green"><xsl:value-of select="."/></font></td>
  </tr>
</xsl:template>

<xsl:template match="line[6]|line[8]">
  <tr>
    <td align="right"><b><i> D</i></b></td>
    <td><font color="purple"><xsl:value-of select="."/></font></td>
  </tr>
</xsl:template>
```

Figure 1.10: `sonnet-html.xsl` (Part 2).

sentence with `<s>` and the end of each sentence with `</s>`. Delete the DOCTYPE line because the DTD does not allow `<s>`. Save the file as sonnet130-sents.xml.

2. Is the file well-formed XML? Use XML plugin to check. Did you find a successful way to fit the `<s>` elements and the `<line>` elements together?

PRACTICAL WORK: CONFLICTING MARKUPS

1. Edit `sonnet13.xml`, shown in Figure 1.13, in the same way. Mark sentence boundaries with `<s>` and `</s>`. Save the file as sonnet13-sents.xml. Is the file well-formed XML? Use XML plugin to check.

```
<xsl:template match="line[9]|line[11]">
  <tr>
    <td align="right"><b><i>E </i></b></td>
    <td><font color="green"><xsl:value-of select="."/></font></td>
  </tr>
</xsl:template>

<xsl:template match="line[10]|line[12]">
  <tr>
    <td align="right"><b><i> F</i></b></td>
    <td><font color="purple"><xsl:value-of select="."/></font></td>
  </tr>
</xsl:template>

<xsl:template match="line[13]|line[14]">
  <tr>
    <td align="right"><b><i>G </i></b></td>
    <td><font color="blue"><xsl:value-of select="."/></font></td>
  </tr>
</xsl:template>

</xsl:stylesheet>
```

Figure 1.11: `sonnet-html.xsl` (Part 3).

2. In Sonnet 13, several sentence boundaries occur in the middle of lines (for example in lines 1, 6, 13, 14). It's impossible to merge the `<s>` and `<line>` elements together satisfactorily in one well-formed XML file. The reason for this is that XML represents *tree* structures, whereas annotations often require *graph* structures. The solution is to use stand-off markup, described in Section 1.6.

1.6   STAND-OFF ANNOTATIONS

A more sophisticated approach is to separate the text and annotations using *stand-off* markup. This allows new annotations to be added without the risk of conflicting with existing annotations. Multiple layers of annotation can be added to the same text. We see an example of adding new layers of annotation in the following practical work.

We will see detailed examples of how stand-off annotations are represented in XML in Chapter 2 and Chapter 4. Several stand-off annotation tools are described in (Ahn et al. 2006). Here we use GATE (Cunningham et al. 2002) with a simple example to demonstrate the basic idea. Further details about GATE as an annotation architecture will be discussed in Chapter 5.

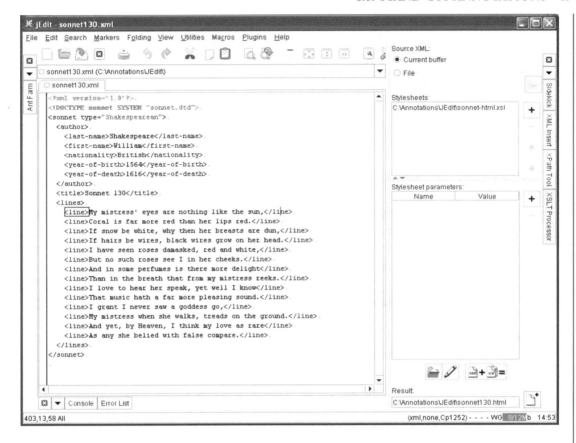

Figure 1.12: Transforming `sonnet130.xml` with jEdit XSLT plugin.

PRACTICAL WORK: STAND-OFF ANNOTATIONS

The GATE website has an online tutorial *Introduction to GATE*, including animations. The tutorial (`http://www.gate.ac.uk/talks/tutorial3`) shows how to load documents into GATE.

1. Load `sonnet130.xml`, the XML version of Sonnet 130, into GATE with a document name *sonnet130.xml* (see *Introduction to GATE: Creating documents*). In detail: Select File → New language resource → GATE document. In the pop-up Parameters window, enter *sonnet130.xml* as Name at the top, and click the browse icon on the right to browse to `sonnet130.xml`.

2. View the text and the XML markup in GATE (see *Introduction to GATE: Inspecting the processing results*). In detail: Double-click *sonnet130.xml* under Language Resources to open a *sonnet130.xml* tab on the right. Click Text to see the text. Click Annotation Sets to see the XML markup (Original markups) and check specific elements to see them highlighted. This is stand-off markup. The text and annotations are separated.

```
<?xml version="1.0"?>
<sonnet type="Shakespearean">
  <author>
    <last-name>Shakespeare</last-name>
    <first-name>William</first-name>
    <nationality>British</nationality>
    <year-of-birth>1564</year-of-birth>
    <year-of-death>1616</year-of-death>
  </author>
  <title>Sonnet 13</title>
  <lines>
    <line>O! that you were your self; but, love you are</line>
    <line>No longer yours, than you your self here live:</line>
    <line>Against this coming end you should prepare,</line>
    <line>And your sweet semblance to some other give:</line>
    <line>So should that beauty which you hold in lease</line>
    <line>Find no determination; then you were</line>
    <line>Yourself again, after yourself's decease,</line>
    <line>When your sweet issue your sweet form should bear.</line>
    <line>Who lets so fair a house fall to decay,</line>
    <line>Which husbandry in honour might uphold,</line>
    <line>Against the stormy gusts of winter's day</line>
    <line>And barren rage of death's eternal cold?</line>
    <line>O! none but unthrifts. Dear my love, you know,</line>
    <line>You had a father: let your son say so.</line>
  </lines>
</sonnet>
```

Figure 1.13: sonnet13.xml: Shakespeare's Sonnet 13 with XML markup.

3. Create a GATE corpus *Sonnet* with only *sonnet130.xml* in it (see *Introduction to GATE: Creating corpora*). In detail: Select File → New language resource → GATE corpus. In the Parameters window, enter *Sonnet* as Name at the top, and click the icon on the right to get a list of documents. Select *sonnet130.xml* and click Add and OK.

4. Load ANNIE "with defaults" (see *Introduction to GATE: ANNIE - a ready-made information extraction system for English*). In detail: Click on the ANNIE menu ("A" icon at the top) and select With defaults.

5. Run ANNIE on the *Sonnet* corpus. In detail: Double-click ANNIE under Applications to open an ANNIE tab on the right. Select the ANNIE tab and click Run.

6. View the new annotations added by ANNIE and the original XML markup (see *Introduction to GATE: Inspecting the processing results*). In detail: Select the *sonnet130.xml* tab and click Annotation Sets. The new annotations should be similar to Figure 1.14.

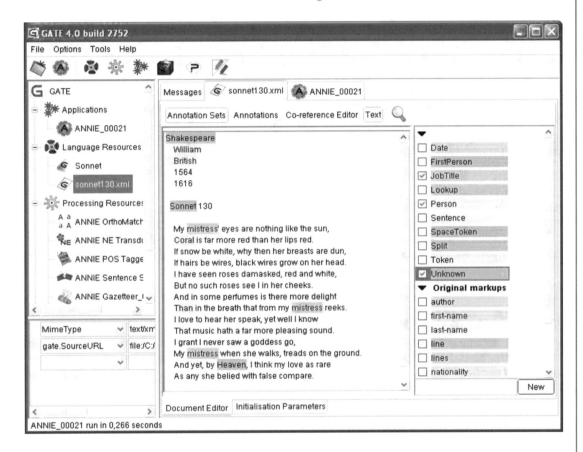

Figure 1.14: GATE: Sonnet 130 with stand-off markups.

7. Note that ANNIE has made three Person annotations: *William British*, *Coral* and *Than*. As the text has been separated from its original markup, ANNIE recognizes *William British* as a plausible Person, and *Coral* as a female Person, but incorrectly marks *Than* as a male Person.

8. Amusingly, ANNIE annotates *mistress* as Job Title (like *schoolmistress*), and marks *Shakespeare*, *Sonnet* and *Heaven* as Unknown. ANNIE "with defaults" is a general-purpose information extraction system, not specifically intended for Shakespearean sonnets. Text analytics systems often need to be specially tailored to different genres - we'll see how to customize GATE gazetteers in Chapter 5.

1.7   ANNOTATION STANDARDS

Practical experience of work with linguistic annotations has given rise to two key recommendations. First: *Use XML*. At least use XML for data interchange, even if you have good reasons for not using it internally in your system. The great advantage of using XML is that whatever specific annotation format you choose now, it can be transformed later if required into other formats by XSLT transformations. Another way of putting this is: *XML means never having to say you're sorry*. This is the topic of Chapter 4, which shows several concrete examples of how to transform one XML annotation format into another.

Second: *Use stand-off annotations*. The great advantage of using stand-off annotations is that whatever specific types of annotation you make now, other types of annotation can be added later, because the original text is still available. Another way of putting this is: *The text is sacred*. Note that when a document is loaded into GATE as in Section 1.6, GATE strips off any existing markup from the text. The text is shown separately in the Text tab, and the markup is shown as *Original markups* in the Annotation Sets tab (Figure 1.14).

XML CORPUS ENCODING STANDARD

Practical experience has also been incorporated into annotation standards. A good overview of standardization efforts for XML-based annotations is given in Robin Cover's *XML Cover Pages* (`http://xml.coverpages.org/`).

The XML Corpus Encoding Standard (XCES) (Ide et al. 2000) is the basic standard for encoding annotated corpora using XML. XCES is an XML version of the earlier Corpus Encoding Standard (CES) (`http://www.cs.vassar.edu/CES/`), which used SGML. CES formed part of the guidelines developed by the Text Encoding Initiative (TEI) and the Expert Advisory Group on Language Engineering Standards (EAGLES).

XML METADATA INTERCHANGE STANDARD

As there are numerous different annotation formats in current use, a standard interchange format has been proposed. XML Metadata Interchange (XMI) is a standard format for interchange of annotations produced by different tools. Chapter 4 explains this format and gives an example of how to transform another XML annotation format into XMI.

1.8   FURTHER READING

The IBM developerWorks website (`http://www.ibm.com/developerworks`) has introductory tutorials on XML, validation with DTDs and XML Schemas, XSLT transformations, and Java programming with XML.

The W3Schools website (`http://www.w3schools.com`) also has introductory tutorials on XML, DTDs, XML Schemas, XPath and XSLT. The XML tutorial includes an XML Quiz, so you can check how much you already know.

- XML editing with jEdit: See (Le Page and Wellens 2003).

- XSLT transformations: See (Tidwell 2001).

- GATE: See (Cunningham et al. 2002).

- Stand-off annotations: See (Ahn et al. 2006).

- XML Corpus Encoding Standard (XCES): See (Ide et al. 2000).

C H A P T E R   2

Linguistic Annotation

In this chapter, we introduce the basic ideas of linguistic annotations and gain practice in doing annotations by hand using a graphical user interface. At the end of the chapter, we will do automatic annotations by way of contrast. Automatic annotations using statistical NLP tools are the topic of Chapter 3.

2.1 LEVELS OF LINGUISTIC ANNOTATION

In linguistic theory, the analysis and description of linguistic phenomena are usually organized into several distinct levels. The different sounds used by a language are described at the level of *phonology*. The writing system is described at the level of *orthography*. *Morphology* describes the formation and inflection of individual words. *Syntax* describes the ordering of words and their combination into phrases and sentences. *Semantics* analyzes the meaning of individual words (*lexical semantics*) and the meaning of phrases and sentences (*compositional semantics*). How words and phrases are actually used to make things happen is the level of *pragmatics*. How people and things are introduced as topics and subsequently referred to in later utterances is the level of *discourse*.

The different levels of linguistic description can be thought of as layers, as shown in Figure 2.1. Phonology and orthography deal with the smallest units (individual sounds and letters) at the bottom. Morphology, syntax and semantics deal with the medium-sized units (words, phrases and sentences). Discourse and pragmatics deal with the largest units (whole paragraphs and dialogues) at the top.

discourse	cohesion in a text or dialogue
pragmatics	functions of utterances
semantics	meaning of words and sentences
syntax	word order and sentence structure
morphology	word formation and inflections
orthography	spelling (written language)
phonology	sounds (spoken language)

Figure 2.1: Levels of linguistic description.

The current state of the art in linguistic annotation also divides the different annotation tasks into different levels, which can be arranged into a similar set of layers as shown in Figure 2.2. However, there is only an approximate correspondence between the levels of the tasks performed in practical corpus annotation work and the levels of description in linguistic theory.

This book focusses on the annotation of texts, where the language is written not spoken, so we do not include an annotation level matching phonology. The annotation tasks that deal with the level of orthography are *tokenization* and *sentence boundary detection*. These tasks segment the text into distinct words (tokens) and distinct sentences. It does not usually matter which of these two tasks is performed first, but it is important that both tasks are performed before the higher-level tasks are done.

coreference resolution	linking references to same entities in a text
named entity recognition	identifying and labeling named entities
semantic analysis	labeling predicate-argument relations
syntactic parsing	analyzing constituent phrases in a sentence
part-of-speech tagging	labeling words with word categories
tokenization	segmenting text into words
sentence boundaries	segmenting text into sentences

Figure 2.2: Levels of linguistic annotations.

After the text has been tokenized into distinct words, each word can be labeled with a word category (Noun, Verb, etc.). This task is *part-of-speech tagging*. It deals with the linguistic level of morphology, as word endings may help to decide the word category. For example, morphology tells us that the ending *-ing* is a morphological unit used with verbs (in English). However, labels must also be given to words without morphological endings. For example, *king* is a noun, and *sing* is a verb. In these words the ending *-ing* is not a separate morphological unit.

After the text has been segmented into sentences, each sentence can be analyzed into its constituent phrases (Noun Phrase, Verb Phrase, etc.). This analysis is *syntactic parsing*, and there is a clear correspondence between the linguistic level (syntax) and the annotation task (syntactic parsing). At this level there are many alternative linguistic theories, and the phrase structure model we will use is just one (widely used) approach. For example, dependency syntax does not use phrases as constituents.

At the higher linguistic levels of semantics, pragmatics and discourse, there are numerous different theories and it is difficult to find a clear consensus for use in the practical tasks of corpus annotation. We will not have much to say about semantics or pragmatics. However, there are linguistic annotation tasks which correspond approximately to the linguistic level of discourse. *Named entity recognition* is the task of identifying entities mentioned in a text and labeling them (Person, Organization, Location, etc.). *Coreference resolution* is the task of working out which references in a text refer to the same entities.

2.2   WORDFREAK ANNOTATION TOOL

There are many tools that can be used for linguistic annotation. We will use WordFreak (http://wordfreak.sourceforge.net/), a Java-based linguistic annotation tool designed to support both human and automatic annotation of linguistic data. WordFreak is briefly described by its developers Thomas Morton and Jeremy LaCivita in (Morton and LaCivita 2003). There is no user manual, so we will give detailed examples here.

We use WordFreak in order to gain practical experience of doing linguistic annotations by hand. That's the only way to learn the difficulties involved in making decisions in linguistic annotations. Later, when we use statistical NLP tools, we will appreciate the speed and power of automatic annotations, by contrast with manual annotations.

As an example text, we will use Shakespeare's Sonnet 130. Figure 2.3 shows sonnet130.txt, a plain text version of Sonnet 130.

WordFreak creates stand-off XML annotations. We will describe the format and see examples in the following sections. Note that GATE and WordFreak deal with existing annotations differently.

```
        Sonnet 130

by William Shakespeare (1564-1616)


My mistress' eyes are nothing like the sun,
Coral is far more red than her lips red.
If snow be white, why then her breasts are dun,
If hairs be wires, black wires grow on her head.
I have seen roses damasked, red and white,
But no such roses see I in her cheeks.
And in some perfumes is there more delight
Than in the breath that from my mistress reeks.
I love to hear her speak, yet well I know
That music hath a far more pleasing sound.
I grant I never saw a goddess go,
My mistress when she walks, treads on the ground.
And yet, by Heaven, I think my love as rare
As any she belied with false compare.
```

Figure 2.3: `sonnet130.txt` Plain text version of Sonnet 130.

GATE strips existing markups from the text and shows them separately as *Original markups*, as described in Section 1.6. WordFreak removes nothing from the text, even existing annotations. That is why we start from the plain text version of the sonnet when using WordFreak.

PRACTICAL WORK: RUNNING WORDFREAK

1. The shell script shown in Figure 2.4 runs WordFreak. Change the value of WORD-FREAK_HOME to the name of the directory where you installed WordFreak. Make the script executable (`chmod +x wordfreak.sh`).

2. Use the script to start WordFreak like this:
   `./wordfreak.sh &`.

PRACTICAL WORK: LOADING A TEXT INTO WORDFREAK

1. To load Sonnet 130 into WordFreak, select Project → Add..., and browse to `sonnet130.txt`.

2. When WordFreak asks "Would you like to create an annotation file?", choose Yes. This creates an annotations (.ann) file `sonnet130.txt.ann`.

3. Press Load and a green tick/check mark should appear, as in Figure 2.5.

4. Save the project as `sonnet130-wordfreak.prj`.

```
#!/bin/sh
# Shell script to run WordFreak 2.2
# G. Wilcock 21.11.2007
#
# Usage: wordfreak.sh &

WORDFREAK_HOME=~gwilcock/Tools/wordfreak-2.2
export WORDFREAK_HOME

java -cp $WORDFREAK_HOME/wordfreak-2.2.jar wordfreak
```

Figure 2.4: `wordfreak.sh`: A shell script to run WordFreak.

2.3   SENTENCE BOUNDARIES

Given a text to be annotated, we can start by dividing it into sentences. This is *sentence boundary detection*, as we detect the boundaries of each sentence: the point in the text where the sentence starts and the point where it ends.

The simplest approach for written language is to split the text at fullstops ("."). However, this is too simple. There are other end-of-sentence markers besides fullstops, such as question marks ("?") and exclamation marks ("!"). More importantly, there are other uses of fullstops that do not mark end-of-sentence, such as in abbreviations ("Mr.", "etc."). There are also situations where a fullstop has more than one function, for example when "etc." is the last word of a sentence, a single fullstop simultaneously marks both the end of the abbreviation and the end of the sentence.

One practical reason for doing sentence boundary detection is that syntactic parsing is normally done on individual sentences rather than complete texts. From a computational point of view, the time required for automatic syntactic parsing tends to grow exponentially as the text length increases, so it is necessary to split the text into shorter units first.

However, this gives rise to a paradox. One of the tasks of syntactic parsing is to tell us whether a given string of words is, or is not, a grammatically correct sentence according to a given grammar. Clearly this task is short-circuited if we decide the sentence boundaries in advance. Ideally, the results of syntactic parsing should play a role in detecting the correct sentence boundaries.

This paradox is not a problem for human annotators. We read the text, parse the sentences, and see the fullstops, all more or less unconsciously. We obviously use our syntactic knowledge to help us decide sentence boundaries.

PRACTICAL WORK: SENTENCE BOUNDARIES IN WORDFREAK

1. Load Sonnet 130 into WordFreak.

2. Select Annotation → Set Annotation → Sentence. This opens a pop-up menu. Some buttons on the menu have navigation icons. Two buttons, labeled *sentence* and *section*, are used to annotate segments of the text.

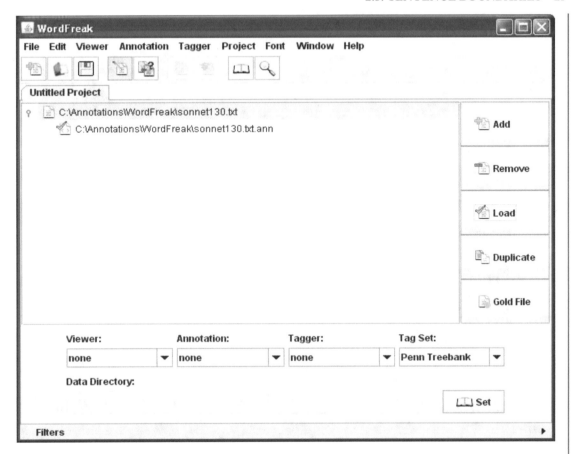

Figure 2.5: Loading Sonnet 130 into WordFreak.

3. Select Viewer → Text and open the Text tab. Click the mouse at a sentence start and drag to the sentence end to highlight the sentence. Click the *sentence* button on the pop-up menu to annotate it as a sentence.

4. Figure 2.6 shows this process. One of the sentences has been selected by the mouse. At the bottom of the window, WordFreak tells us that the annotations are stored in the file sonnet130.txt.ann, the annotator of the highlighted item was "gw" (a human annotator), the highlighted item is a sentence, and it starts at position 69 and ends at position 155.

5. Mark all the sentences. Save the project and view the XML annotations in the .ann file. They should look something like Figure 2.7.

The WordFreak annotation format in Figure 2.7 has Annotation elements for every type of annotation. There is one file annotation with type="file", which gives the file's start index (0) and end index (691) in the form span="0..691" and also gives the file's name. Sentence annotations have

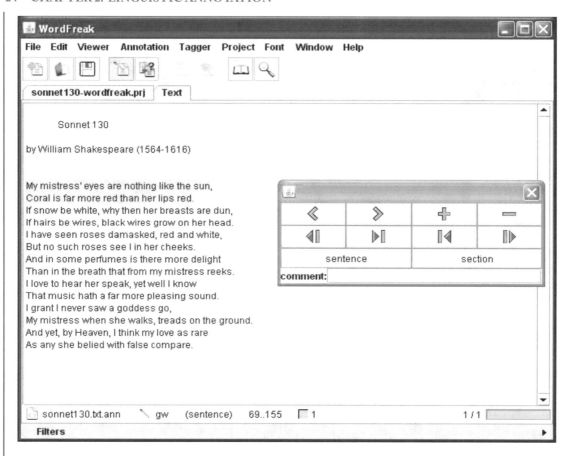

Figure 2.6: Marking sentence boundaries with WordFreak.

type="sentence" and are nested inside the file annotation. Each sentence's start and end indices are given in its span attribute. The annotator is named for each annotation. In this example, each sentence annotation was made by "gw" (a human annotator).

2.4   TOKENIZATION

Given a text to be annotated, another way to start is by dividing it into words. Of course, the same word may occur many times in a text, and we say that this "same word" is a word *type* and each separate occurrence of it is a word *token*. The task of identifying the tokens is called *tokenization*. We decide the boundaries of each token: the point in the text where the token starts and the point where it ends.

In general, either sentence boundary detection or tokenization can be done first. They are usually the two first stages in annotating a text, as their results are used by later stages. Sentences are the input units for syntactic parsing, and word tokens are the input units for part-of-speech tagging.

```
<?xml version="1.0" encoding="UTF-8"?>
<AnnotationFile version="2.4">
 <features list="filename,annotator"/>
 <annotators list="tagger,gw"/>
 <Annotation type="file" span="0..691" confidence="0.0" id="1"
  filename="C:\Annotations\sonnet130.txt.ann" annotator="tagger">
  <Annotation type="sentence" span="14..64"
    confidence="1.0" id="2" annotator="gw"/>
  <Annotation type="sentence" span="69..155"
    confidence="1.0" id="3" annotator="gw"/>
  <Annotation type="sentence" span="156..254"
    confidence="1.0" id="4" annotator="gw"/>
  <Annotation type="sentence" span="255..338"
    confidence="1.0" id="5" annotator="gw"/>
  <Annotation type="sentence" span="339..431"
    confidence="1.0" id="6" annotator="gw"/>
  <Annotation type="sentence" span="432..518"
    confidence="1.0" id="7" annotator="gw"/>
  <Annotation type="sentence" span="519..604"
    confidence="1.0" id="8" annotator="gw"/>
  <Annotation type="sentence" span="605..688"
    confidence="1.0" id="9" annotator="gw"/>
 </Annotation>
</AnnotationFile>
```

Figure 2.7: WordFreak annotation format: sentences.

The simplest approach to tokenization for written language is to split the text at whitespace (spaces, tabs and newlines). However, this is too simple. For the last sentence, this gives tokens such as "However," (including the comma), and "simple." (including the fullstop). So we usually consider the punctuation as separate tokens, giving "simple" as one token and "." as another token.

In general this works well, but in some specific cases it's better to include punctuation as part of a token. For example, we may decide to count "Mr." as one token (including the fullstop). This seems to work well, but other cases are difficult. If we similarly decide that "etc." is one token (including the fullstop), that means that a sentence ending with "etc." does not have the fullstop as its end-of-sentence marker.

We may consider the possessive ending "'s" to be a single token (including the apostrophe). Again, this is a paradox, like deciding sentence boundaries before doing syntactic parsing. It is the task of the part-of-speech tagging stage to label the tokens, and to decide whether "'s" is the possessive ending (POS) or not. If we already decide that this is a single token in the tokenization stage, the part-of-speech tagging is short-circuited. Sometimes "'s" is not the possessive ending, for example "it's" is a contraction of "it is".

PRACTICAL WORK: TOKENIZATION IN WORDFREAK

1. Load Sonnet 130 into WordFreak, and mark sentence boundaries.

2. Select Annotation → Set Annotation → Token. Select Viewer → Text. Select Tagger → Set Tagger → Simple Token. Figure 2.8 shows this step.

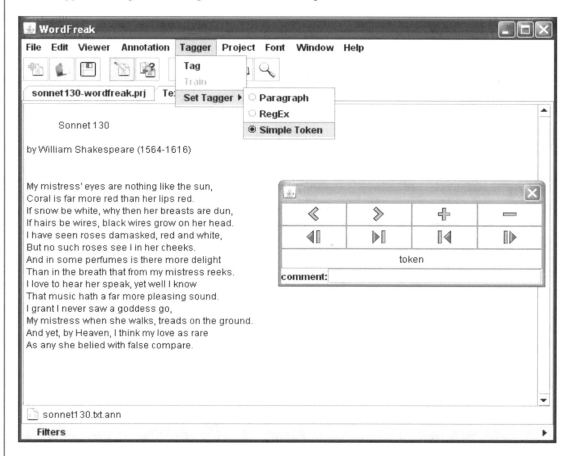

Figure 2.8: Selecting the simple tokenizer in WordFreak.

3. Click Tagger → Tag to do automatic tokenization. Figure 2.9 shows the results. One of the tokens, *belied*, has been selected by the mouse. At the bottom of the window, WordFreak tells us that the annotator of the highlighted item was "tagger" (an automatic tagger), the highlighted item is a token, and it starts at position 661 and ends at position 667.

4. Note that you can navigate within the text viewer using the buttons in the pop-up menu. For example, use < to move left and > to move right. The navigation is context-sensitive: if you are viewing tokens you move to the next token, if you are viewing sentences you move to the next sentence. You can also use the arrow keys on your keyboard.

5. Save the project and view the XML annotations.

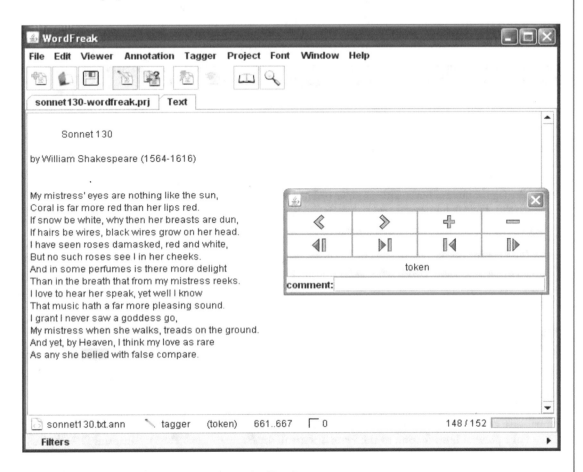

Figure 2.9: After simple tokenization in WordFreak.

2.5   PART-OF-SPEECH TAGGING

The task of part-of-speech tagging is to label every token with a part-of-speech label. Traditionally there are eight parts of speech for English: Noun (N), Verb (V), Adjective (A or Adj), Adverb (Adv), Preposition (P), Article or Determiner (Det), Conjunction (Conj) and Interjection (Int). Many other alternative classifications have been proposed.

In linguistic theory, these basic categories have been further divided into subcategories. Nouns are subdivided into proper nouns (*John, Mary, Helsinki*), common nouns (*man, woman, city*), and pronouns (*he, she, it*). Verbs are subdivided into intransitive verbs (*walk*, with no object), transitive verbs (*see*, with one object), and ditransitive verbs (*give*, with two objects). Adjectives are subdivided into absolute (*big*), comparative (*bigger*), and superlative (*biggest*).

Another way to distinguish different categories is by using *features*. Nouns (N) can be labeled N(singular) (*man, woman, city*), or N(plural) (*men, women, cities*). Verbs (V) can be labeled V(past) (*walked, saw, gave*), or V(present) (*walk, see, give*). Multiple feature combinations can be used, for example V(present, 3rd-singular) (*walks, sees, gives*).

For the task of part-of-speech tagging, the traditional eight categories appear to miss important distinctions, but multiple feature combinations appear to be too complex. Practical work has used fixed sets of tags, known as *tagsets*, that encode important distinctions but restrict the tag names to atomic values.

THE PENN TREEBANK TAGSET

One of the more popular tagsets is the Penn Treebank tagset, used for the Penn Treebank project at University of Pennsylvania. A list of the tags in the Penn Treebank tagset is shown in Figure 2.10.

In the Penn Treebank tagset, there are six different tags for verbs: VB, VBZ, VBP, VBD, VBN, VBG. The tag for present tense, 3rd-singular verbs (*walks, sees, gives*) is VBZ (Z sounds like the ending of *sees* and *gives*). The tag for present tense, non-3rd-singular verbs (*walk, see, give*) is VBP (P means present). The tag for past tense (*walked, saw, gave*) is VBD (D is the ending of regular past tense verbs like *walked*). The tag for past participle (*walked, seen, given*) is VBN (N is the ending of many past participles like *seen, given*). The tag for present participle (*walking, seeing, giving*) is VBG (G is the ending of *-ing*). The tag for the base form of verbs (*walk, see, give*) is VB (the base form has no ending). The difference between VB and VBP is that VB is the infinitive form used with *to*, like *be* in *to be*, and VBP is the present tense form used with *you*, like *are* in *you are*.

Nouns have several different tags. A singular common noun (*city*) is NN. A plural common noun (*cities*) is NNS (S is the ending of regular plurals like *cities*). A singular proper noun (*Helsinki*) is NNP (here, P means proper). A plural proper noun (*Helsinkis*) is NNPS. A personal pronoun (*he, she, it*) is PRP. A possessive pronoun (*his, her, its*) is PRP$ ($ is vaguely like the S ending of *his, its*).

A basic adjective (*big*) is JJ (J is the ending of Adj). A comparative adjective (*bigger*) is JJR (R is the ending of *-er*). A superlative adjective (*biggest*) is JJS (here, S means superlative). A basic adverb (*badly*) is RB (RB is the ending of Adverb). A comparative adverb (*worse*) is RBR (R is the ending of regular comparative adverbs like *better*). A superlative adverb (*worst*) is RBS (S for superlative).

For a general introduction to the Penn Treebank see (Marcus et al. 1993). Santorini (1990) gives detailed guidelines on using the Penn Treebank tagset.

WordFreak was developed at University of Pennsylvania, and provides pop-up menus for the Penn Treebank tagset. These menus are very useful when doing POS tagging by hand with this tagset. The tags in Figure 2.10 are listed in the same order as the WordFreak pop-up menu shown in Figure 2.11.

PRACTICAL WORK: PART-OF-SPEECH TAGGING IN WORDFREAK

1. Continue with Sonnet 130 loaded in WordFreak, already tokenized.

2. Select Annotation → Set Annotation → POS. This opens a pop-up menu with buttons for the part-of-speech tags as shown in Figure 2.11.

3. Select Viewer → TextPOS. In the TextPOS viewer, the part-of-speech tags will be shown above the words. For example, *Sonnet* is a noun (NN) and *130* is a cardinal number (CD). If the word is short and the tag is too long to fit over it, an underscore is shown instead.

4. Using the menus, do POS tagging by hand for several lines of the sonnet. Figure 2.11 shows the procedure. One of the tokens, *are*, has been selected by the mouse. At the bottom of the window,

VB	Verb, base form	*be, hear*
VBZ	Verb, 3rd person singular present	*is, reeks*
VBP	Verb, non-3rd person singular present	*are, grow*
VBD	Verb, past tense	*saw*
VBN	Verb, past participle	*seen, belied*
VBG	Verb, present participle	
RP	Particle	
-LRB-	Left round bracket/parenthesis	*(*
-RRB-	Right round bracket/parenthesis	*)*
NN	Noun, singular	*sonnet*
NNS	Noun, plural	*eyes*
IN	Preposition	*by, on*
DT	Determiner	*the, any*
TO	*to*	*to*
CC	Coordinating conjunction	*and*
#	(currency), Pound sign	*#*
MD	Modal verb	*should*
JJ	Adjective	*red, white*
JJR	Adjective, comparative	*redder*
JJS	Adjective, superlative	*reddest*
RB	Adverb	*well, never*
RBR	Adverb, comparative	*more*
RBS	Adverb, superlative	*most*
PRP	Personal pronoun	*I, she*
PRP$	Possessive pronoun	*my, her*
NNP	Proper noun, singular	*William*
NNPS	Proper noun, plural	
LS	List item	
EX	Existential *there*	*there*
PDT	Predeterminer	*all*
SYM	Symbol	
CD	Cardinal number	*130*
.	(punctuation), End of sentence	*.*
,	(punctuation), Comma	*,*
:	(punctuation), Middle of sentence	*;*
”	(punctuation), Right quotation marks	*”*
continues		

continued		
"	(punctuation), Left quotation marks	"
$	(currency), Dollar sign	$
UH	Interjection	O!
POS	Possessive ending	's, '
FW	Foreign word	
WP	*wh*-Pronoun	*who*
WP$	Possessive *wh*-pronoun	*whose*
WRB	*wh*-Adverb	*when*
WDT	*wh*-Determiner	*what*
HYPH	Hyphen	–
AFX	Affix	

Figure 2.10: WordFreak/Penn Treebank part-of-speech tagset.

WordFreak tells us that the annotator of the highlighted item was "gw", the highlighted item is a VBP, and it starts at position 87 and ends at position 90.

5. Save the project and view the XML annotations in the .ann file. The POS annotations for the title and author information should look something like Figure 2.12.

The WordFreak annotation format in Figure 2.12 shows POS tag annotations for the sonnet's title ("Sonnet 130 by William Shakespeare (1564-1616)"). They are nested inside the sentence annotation for the sentence containing the words. The type attribute of each POS tag annotation gives the POS tag, for example the POS tag annotation for a noun has type="NN". When a token has not been tagged with a POS tag, its type is token, as in the second sentence. Each POS tag's start and end indices are given in its span attribute. The annotator is named for each annotation. In this example, each POS annotation was made by "gw" (a human annotator).

Note that the WordFreak annotation format in Figure 2.12 does not include the words themselves, only their start and end points. In Chapter 4 we will use an XSLT transformation to add the words to the annotations.

2.6   SYNTACTIC PARSING

The task of syntactic parsing is to analyze sentence structures. The kind of structures that are identified depends on the grammatical theory being used. For example, dependency grammars use graph structures to show dependency relationships between words, while phrase structure grammars use tree structures to show constituency relationships between phrases.

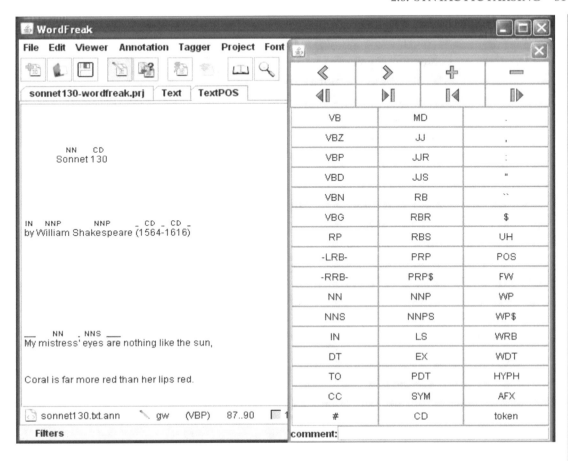

Figure 2.11: Part-of-speech tagging in WordFreak.

We will use phrase structure grammars. This is the approach used by the Penn Treebank and WordFreak, and also by the statistical NLP tools that we will use in Chapter 3. In parsing with a phrase structure grammar, the words in a sentence are grouped into phrases, and the phrases form constituents of longer phrases and of sentences. A good introduction to syntactic theory and phrase structure grammars is given by (Sag et al. 2003).

There are different kinds of phrases, based on different word categories. For example, a noun phrase (NP) is based on a noun, a verb phrase (VP) is based on a verb, and a prepositional phrase (PP) is based on a preposition. The word on which the phrase is based is called the head word of the phrase.

Note that the word categories used for part-of-speech tagging in Section 2.5 distinguish different subcategories of noun: singular common noun (NN), plural common noun (NNS), singular proper noun (NNP), plural proper noun (NNPS), etc. A noun phrase must be based on a noun, but it can be any of these different subcategories of noun. Similarly, a verb phrase can be based on any of the different subcategories of verb: VBP, VBZ, VBD, VBN, VBG, etc.

```
...
<Annotation type="sentence" span="14..64"
  confidence="1.0" id="2" annotator="gw">
 <Annotation type="NN" span="15..21"
   confidence="1.0" id="3" annotator="gw"/>
 <Annotation type="CD" span="22..25"
   confidence="1.0" id="4" annotator="gw"/>
 <Annotation type="IN" span="29..31"
   confidence="1.0" id="5" annotator="gw"/>
 <Annotation type="NNP" span="32..39"
   confidence="1.0" id="6" annotator="gw"/>
 <Annotation type="NNP" span="40..51"
   confidence="1.0" id="7" annotator="gw"/>
 <Annotation type="-LRB-" span="52..53"
   confidence="1.0" id="8" annotator="gw"/>
 <Annotation type="CD" span="53..57"
   confidence="1.0" id="9" annotator="gw"/>
 <Annotation type=":" span="57..58"
   confidence="1.0" id="10" annotator="gw"/>
 <Annotation type="CD" span="58..62"
   confidence="1.0" id="11" annotator="gw"/>
 <Annotation type="-RRB-" span="62..63"
   confidence="1.0" id="12" annotator="gw"/>
</Annotation>
<Annotation type="sentence" span="69..155"
  confidence="1.0" id="13" annotator="gw">
 <Annotation type="token" span="69..71"
   confidence="0.0" id="14" annotator="tagger"/>
...
```

Figure 2.12: WordFreak annotation format: POS tags.

Phrase structure rules specify how a head word can be combined with other words to make a phrase. For example, a noun phrase (NP) can be made by combining a determiner (DT) and a noun, as in *the cat*. A head word may also be combined with a phrase to make a longer phrase. For example a preposition is combined with a noun phrase to make a prepositional phrase (PP): *on* is a preposition, *the mat* is a noun phrase, and *on the mat* is a prepositional phrase. One way that a verb phrase (VP) can be made is by combining a verb with a prepositional phrase: *sat* is a verb (VBD), *on the mat* is a prepositional phrase, and *sat on the mat* is a verb phrase. A noun phrase can be combined with a verb phrase to make a sentence (S): *the cat* is a noun phrase, *sat on the mat* is a verb phrase, and *the cat sat on the mat* is a sentence.

The way that phrases form constituents of longer phrases is often shown by a parse tree diagram as in Figure 2.13.

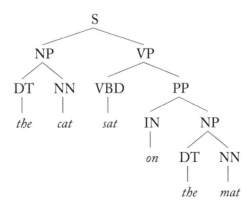

Figure 2.13: A syntactic parse tree.

For annotation purposes, the labels (NP, VP, PP, S, etc.) of the different kinds of phrases are a tagset, called a syntactic constituent tagset. With WordFreak, we use the constituent tagset shown in Figure 2.14, based on the Penn Treebank syntactic tagset described in (Marcus et al. 1993).

As well as full syntactic parsing, there is a limited form of parsing that only checks for noun phrases (or another specific phrase type). This is called *chunking* or *partial parsing*, and is used in automatic annotation as a step towards named entity recognition. Chunking is described further in Chapter 3.

PRACTICAL WORK: SYNTACTIC PARSING IN WORDFREAK

1. Continue with Sonnet 130 loaded in WordFreak, already tagged.

2. Select Annotation → Set Annotation → Constituent. This opens a pop-up menu for syntactic constituents as shown in Figure 2.15

3. Select Viewer → Tree. The Tree viewer gives a Java Tree view of the syntactic constituency tree. Nodes can be opened (expanded) or closed (contracted) by mouse clicks. Higher-level constituents can be labeled before or after labeling the lower-level units inside them.

4. Use the mouse to highlight a section of the tree, and use the menu to label it with a constituent label. Mark noun phrases (NP), prepositional phrases (PP), verb phrases (VP) and sentences (S) in the sonnet. Save the project and view the annotations.

2.7   SEMANTICS AND DISCOURSE

The higher linguistic levels of semantics, pragmatics and discourse mentioned in Section 2.1 are subjects of current research and are less well-understood than the more concrete levels of phonology, morphology and syntax. We will mention only three topics: predicate-argument analysis, discourse connectives, and coreference.

NP	Noun Phrase	*My mistress' eyes*
ADVP	Adverb Phrase	*far more*
SQ	Inverted yes/no question	
INTJ	Interjection	
S	Sentence (simple declarative clause)	
SINV	Inverted declarative sentence	*in some perfumes is there …*
X	Unknown or uncertain category	
WHADJP	*wh*-Adjective Phrase	
SBAR	Subordinate Clause	*if snow be white*
NX	Head of NP	
RRC	Reduced Relative Clause	*belied with false compare*
CONJP	Conjunction Phrase	
VP	Verb Phrase	*are nothing like the sun*
FRAG	Fragment	
QP	Quantifier Phrase (in NP)	
PRT	Particle	
ADJP	Adjective Phrase	*far more red*
UCP	Unlike Coordinated Phrase	
NAC	Not a Constituent	
TOP	Top node of tree	
PRN	Parenthetical	
SBARQ	Question with *wh*-word	
WHADVP	*wh*-Adverb Phrase	*when she walks*
WHPP	*wh*-Prepositional Phrase	
PP	Prepositional Phrase	*on her head*
WHNP	*wh*-Noun Phrase	
LST	List marker	
NML	Nominal modifier (in NP)	*My*

Figure 2.14: WordFreak/Penn Treebank syntactic tagset.

PREDICATE-ARGUMENT ANALYSIS

There are various different semantic theories in linguistics and in philosophy. The idea of basing semantic representations on predicate logic is common to most of them. This requires the identification of predicates and the assignment of the correct arguments to the predicates.

Part of the Penn Treebank has been annotated with predicate-argument relations by the Penn Prop-Bank (Proposition Bank) project. This will facilitate the development of automatic predicate-argument analysis tools. The project is described by (Palmer et al. 2005).

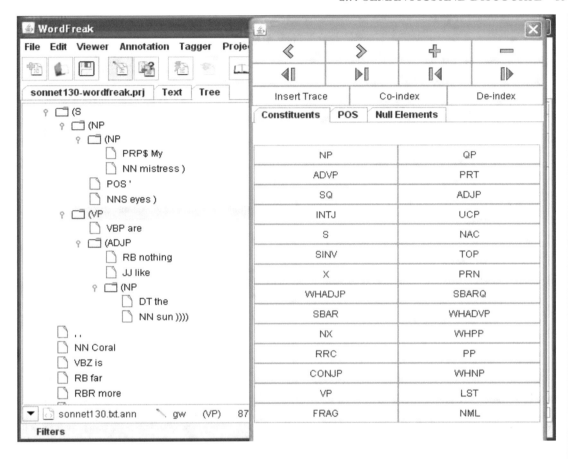

Figure 2.15: Syntactic parsing in WordFreak.

WordFreak supports predicate-argument analysis. In the basic form shown in Figure 2.16, predicate-argument relations are simple triples of verb, subject, object roles. Verb phrases (VPs) are candidates for verb roles, and noun phrases (NPs) are candidates for subject and object roles. In Figure 2.16, *she* has been selected as the Subject argument of the predicate *walks*, and *My mistress* has been selected as the Subject argument of the predicate *treads on the ground*.

PRACTICAL WORK: PREDICATE-ARGUMENT ANALYSIS IN WORDFREAK

1. Continue with Sonnet 130 loaded in WordFreak, already parsed.

2. Select Annotation → Set Annotation → PredArg. This opens a pop-up window for annotating predicate-argument relations as in Figure 2.16. The pop-up window gives a Java Tree view of parts of the text.

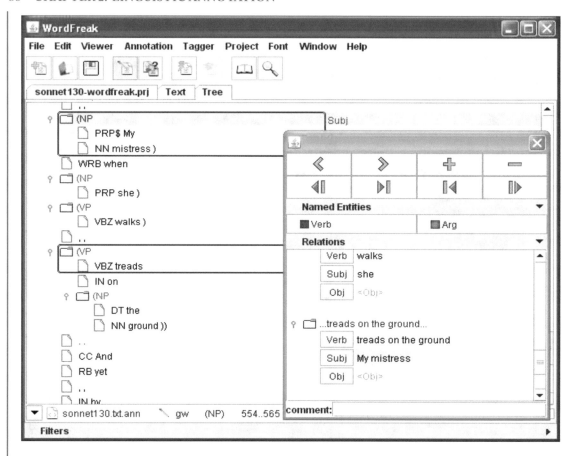

Figure 2.16: Predicate-argument annotation in WordFreak.

3. Select Viewer → Tree. This gives a Java Tree view of the parse tree. In the parse tree, NP nodes and VP nodes are highlighted as candidates for roles in predicate-argument relations.

4. When an NP node is selected in the parse tree, clicking on Subj or Obj in the Relations tree annotates the NP as the subject or object of the given predicate. When a VP node is selected in the parse tree, clicking on Verb in the Relations tree annotates the VP as the predicate of the given subject or object.

5. Identify predicates and their arguments in Sonnet 130.

DISCOURSE CONNECTIVES

Discourse connectives are words like *because* and *however* that indicate the connections between different clauses of a text at the level of discourse coherence. Discourse connectives in the Penn Treebank have been annotated by the Penn Discourse Treebank project. This work, which builds on both the syntactic annotations of the Penn Treebank and the semantic annotations of the Penn PropBank, is described by (Miltsakaki et al. 2004).

COREFERENCE

Coreference occurs when the same entity is referred to more than once. This happens constantly when pronouns like *she* and *her* are used instead of repeating longer phrases like *my mistress*. Coreference also occurs when the same person is referred to by different descriptive expressions, perhaps emphasizing some particular attribute of the person. Of course it also occurs when the same person is referred to more than once by the same expression, as in the case of *my mistress* being repeated in the sonnet.

WordFreak supports coreference annotation. Noun phrases (NPs) are highlighted as candidates for coreference. In Figure 2.17, the NP *My mistress* has been annotated as a new reference, receiving reference number #1. The NP *she* is subsequently annotated as a coreference of *My mistress*, so it is also assigned reference number #1.

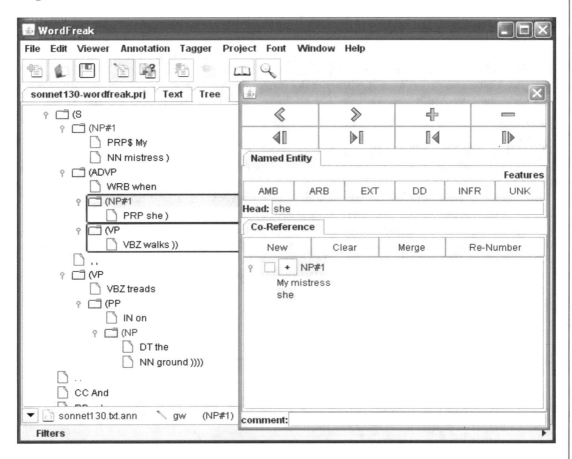

Figure 2.17: Coreference annotation in WordFreak.

PRACTICAL WORK: COREFERENCE ANNOTATION IN WORDFREAK

1. Continue with Sonnet 130 loaded in WordFreak, already parsed.

2. Select Annotation → Set Annotation → NPCoref. This opens a pop-up window for annotating coreference as in Figure 2.17.

3. Select Viewer → Tree. This gives a Java Tree view of the parse tree.

4. When an NP node is selected in the parse tree, clicking New in the Coreference window annotates the NP with a new reference number. When a second NP node is selected in the parse tree, clicking on the plus sign next to an existing reference in the Coreference window adds the second NP as a coreference of the first NP.

5. Identify new references and coreferences in Sonnet 130.

2.8   WORDFREAK WITH OPENNLP

We have learned in the practical work that doing linguistic annotations by hand is a slow process. In this section we combine WordFreak with automatic tagging and parsing tools to do linguistic annotations much faster. We will learn more about statistical annotation tools in Chapter 3.

Automatic annotation tools inevitably make some mistakes, but the errors can be corrected by hand using the WordFreak user interface. The combination of high-speed automatic annotation and high-quality human checking and correction can be a good solution for some annotation tasks.

WORDFREAK OPENNLP PLUGIN

WordFreak OpenNLP Plugin (`http://wordfreak.sourceforge.net/plugins.html`) enables WordFreak to be used together with OpenNLP tools.

There is a small technical complication in setting up WordFreak so it can use the OpenNLP plugin, but it is easily fixed. The OpenNLP plugin is based on an older version of OpenNLP, so the directory names and file names for the OpenNLP model files are slightly different. To make the plugin work, create a subdirectory `models/english/postag`. Copy `tag.bin.gz` from `models/english/parser` to `models/english/postag`, renaming it `EnglishPOS.bin.gz`. Also copy `models/english/parser/tagdict` to `models/english/postag/tagdict`.

PRACTICAL WORK: WORDFREAK WITH OPENNLP PLUGIN

1. The shell script in Figure 2.18 runs WordFreak with the OpenNLP plugin. Change WORD-FREAK_HOME to the name of the directory where you installed WordFreak. Put the jar files from WordFreak OpenNLP plugin in the WORDFREAK_HOME directory. Change OPENNLP_HOME to the name of the directory where you installed OpenNLP. The script sets WordFreak's Data Directory to $OPENNLP_HOME/models/english in order to use the OpenNLP statistical models. Make the script executable (`chmod +x wordfreak-opennlp.sh`).

2. Use the script to start WordFreak like this:
   `./wordfreak-opennlp.sh &`.

3. Load sonnet130.txt into WordFreak, creating an annotations (.ann) file. Save the project as a new project sonnet130-opennlp.prj. After each step below, view the annotations in the viewer tab and in the .ann file.

```
#!/bin/sh
# Shell script to run WordFreak 2.2 with OpenNLP 1.1.
# Uses maxent models from OpenNLP 1.3.0
# G. Wilcock 10.11.2007

WORDFREAK_HOME=~gwilcock/Tools/wordfreak-2.2
export WORDFREAK_HOME

OPENNLP_HOME=~gwilcock/Tools/opennlp-1.3.0
export OPENNLP_HOME

java -Xmx1024m -cp $WORDFREAK_HOME/wordfreak-2.2.jar:\
$WORDFREAK_HOME/opennlp-wordfreak-plugin-1.1.jar:\
$WORDFREAK_HOME/opennlp-tools-1.1.0.jar:\
$WORDFREAK_HOME/maxent-2.3.0.jar:\
$WORDFREAK_HOME/trove.jar \
wordfreak \
-d $OPENNLP_HOME/models/english
```

Figure 2.18: `wordfreak-opennlp.sh`: A shell script to run WordFreak with OpenNLP plugin.

PRACTICAL WORK: SENTENCE DETECTION

1. Select Annotation → Set Annotation → Sentence. Select Viewer → Text. Select Tagger → Set Tagger → Open Sentence (for the OpenNLP Sentence Detector).

2. Figure 2.19 shows this step. When WordFreak is used with OpenNLP plugin, the Set Tagger menu contains many more components than in Figure 2.8. The Data Directory is set to the directory containing the OpenNLP statistical models.

3. Click Tagger → Tag to mark sentence boundaries automatically.

4. Figure 2.20 shows the result of automatic sentence segmentation. At the bottom of the window, WordFreak tells us that the annotations are stored in the file sonnet130.txt.ann, the annotator of the highlighted item was "tagger" (an automatic tagger), the highlighted item is a sentence, and it starts at position 0 and ends at position 155.

5. Note that as there is no full stop between the headings and the start of the sonnet, the headings have been included as part of the first sentence.

PRACTICAL WORK: TOKENIZATION AND POS TAGGING

1. Select Annotation → Set Annotation → Token. Select Viewer → Text. Select Tagger → Set Tagger → Open Token (for the OpenNLP Tokenizer). Click Tagger → Tag to do automatic tokenization. Save the project.

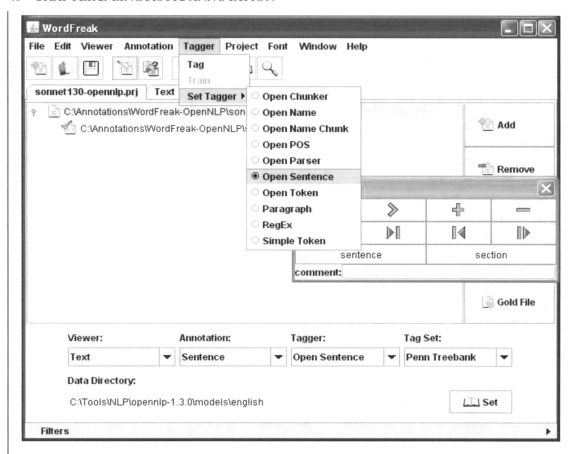

Figure 2.19: WordFreak with OpenNLP plugin.

2. Select Annotation → Set Annotation → POS. Select Viewer → TextPOS. Select Tagger → Set Tagger → Open POS (for the OpenNLP POS Tagger). Click Tagger → Tag to do automatic POS tagging. Save the project.

3. Figure 2.21 shows the result of automatic POS tagging. One of the tokens, *belied*, has been selected by the mouse. At the bottom of the window, WordFreak tells us that the annotator of the highlighted item was "tagger" (an automatic tagger), the highlighted item is a VBN, and it starts at position 661 and ends at position 667.

PRACTICAL WORK: CHUNKING AND PARSING

1. Select Annotation → Set Annotation → Constituent. Select Viewer → Tree. Select Tagger → Set Tagger → Open Chunker (for the OpenNLP Chunker). Click Tagger → Tag to do automatic noun phrase chunking.

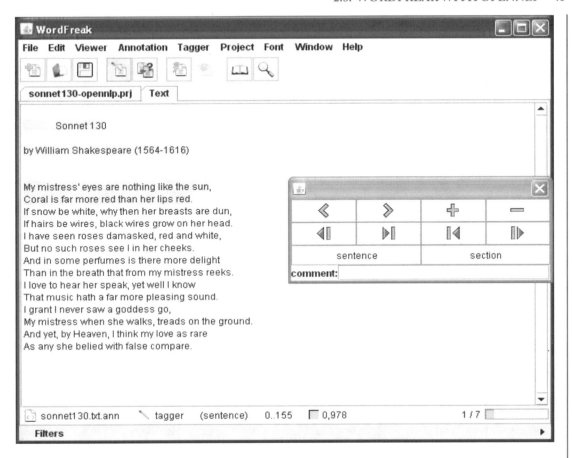

Figure 2.20: Automatic sentence boundaries with WordFreak OpenNLP plugin.

2. Figure 2.22 shows the result of automatic NP chunking. One of the chunks, *Coral*, has been selected by the mouse. WordFreak tells us that the annotator of the highlighted item was "tagger", the highlighted item is an NP, and it starts at position 114 and ends at position 119.

3. Select Annotation → Set Annotation → Constituent. Select Viewer → Tree. Select Tagger → Set Tagger → Open Parser (for the OpenNLP Parser). Click Tagger → Tag to do automatic parsing. Save the project.

4. Figure 2.23 shows the result of automatic parsing. The parser did not find complete parses for the sentences, but did find some constituents. One of the phrases, *far more*, has been selected by the mouse. WordFreak tells us that the annotator was "tagger", the highlighted item is an ADVP, and it starts at position 121 and ends at position 131.

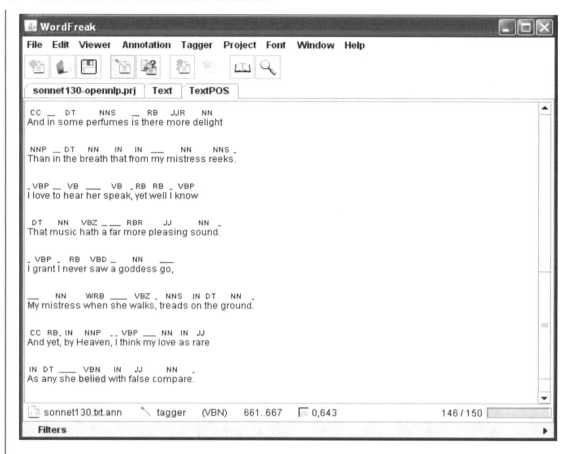

Figure 2.21: Automatic POS tagging with WordFreak OpenNLP plugin.

2.9   FURTHER READING

- Current issues in linguistic annotation: See (Boguraev et al. 2007).

- Sentence boundaries and tokenization: See (Manning and Schütze 1999) Chapter 4.2.

- Part-of-speech tagging: See (Jurafsky and Martin 2008) Chapter 5 and (Manning and Schütze 1999) Chapter 3.1.

- Penn Treebank tagset: See (Santorini 1990).

- Syntactic theory: See (Sag et al. 2003).

- Syntactic parsing: See (Jurafsky and Martin 2008) Chapter 13 and
  (Manning and Schütze 1999) Chapter 3.2.

- WordFreak: See (Morton and LaCivita 2003).

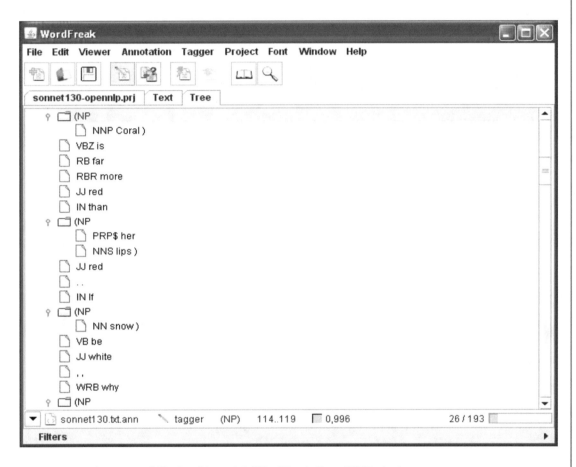

Figure 2.22: Automatic NP chunking with WordFreak OpenNLP plugin.

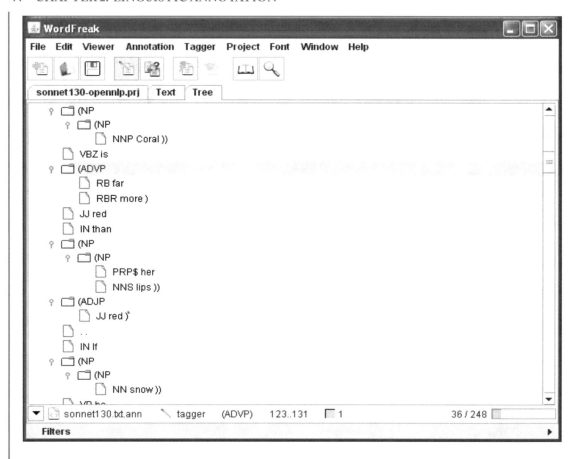

Figure 2.23: Automatic parsing with WordFreak OpenNLP plugin.

CHAPTER 3

Using Statistical NLP Tools

In Chapter 2, we saw that doing linguistic annotations by hand is a slow process, even when using a tool such as WordFreak. In this chapter, we use statistical NLP tools to do linguistic annotations much faster.

Although there is a great contrast in speed between manual and automatic annotations, it does not necessarily follow that automatic annotations are greatly inferior in accuracy. The statistical tools are trained using human annotations. The basic idea is that they will produce annotations as close as possible to the human annotations in similar cases. So in theory, if the text to be annotated is sufficiently similar to the texts used for training, the automatic annotations will be quite similar to human annotations. In practice, this works pretty well at the lower levels such as tokenization and part-of-speech tagging. It does not yet work so well at the higher levels such as syntactic parsing.

3.1   STATISTICAL MODELS

Statistical NLP tools work by using statistical models of significant features relevant to the linguistic level at which they operate. In most cases, the basic approach is *classification*. Classification problems can be solved by *machine learning* methods (Mitchell 1997).

The various NLP tasks are formulated as classification problems, where each case has to be classified as a member of two or more distinct classes. For example, sentence boundary detection is formulated as the task of classifying every fullstop in a text as either (A) a sentence boundary, or (B) not a sentence boundary. Part-of-speech tagging is the task of classifying every token as (A) a member of the class "NN", or (B) a member of the class "NNS", or (C) a member of the class "NNP", and so on for a fixed set of POS tag classes.

The machine learning approach to classification problems has three steps. First, you *train* a statistical model using a large number of examples of cases which have already been correctly classified (this form of learning is *supervised learning* based on examples). Second, you *test* the trained model using a smaller number of examples, which have already been correctly classified but were not used during the training step. Finally, if the testing shows that the trained model performs the classification with the required level of accuracy, you use the trained and tested model to classify new cases, thereby performing the NLP task for which the model was developed.

Many different statistical models and methods have been investigated by researchers in machine learning. Among the more widely-used classification algorithms are different varieties of Naive Bayes classifiers, Decision Tree classifiers, K Nearest Neighbour classifiers and Maximum Entropy classifiers. A good collection of classification algorithms is available in the WEKA machine learning toolkit (`http://www.cs.waikato.ac.nz/~ml/weka`). Like the NLP tools in this book, the WEKA toolkit is free, open source, and implemented in Java. Data mining with WEKA is described in detail in (Witten and Frank 2005).

During the last 10 years or so, one of the most effective statistical modeling approaches in NLP has been the use of maximum entropy models. Maximum entropy models are trained with training files of example cases, and are then used to perform classification tasks based on the examples. From a theoretical point of view, maximum entropy models avoid some of the independence assumptions about the features used in training that are assumed in other models such as Naive Bayes. From a practical point of view, maximum entropy models have been found to work well on a range of NLP tasks.

Ratnaparkhi (1997) describes maximum entropy models and their application to natural language processing. The availability of a good open source Java implementation of maximum entropy models (`http://maxent.sourceforge.net`) has facilitated the implementation of numerous open source Java statistical NLP tools based on Ratnaparkhi's work.

3.2   OPENNLP AND STANFORD NLP TOOLS

We will mainly use statistical NLP tools from the OpenNLP project, but for some tasks (tagging, parsing, and named entity recognition) we also describe the Stanford NLP tools in order to provide a comparison.

OPENNLP TOOLS
The OpenNLP tools (`http://opennlp.sourceforge.net`) are statistical NLP tools including a sentence boundary detector, a tokenizer, a POS tagger, a phrase chunker, a sentence parser, a name finder and a coreference resolver. The tools are based on maximum entropy models and are written in Java.

The OpenNLP tools can be used by themselves, or as plugins with other Java frameworks including WordFreak and UIMA. When the tools are used by themselves, the output is in a simple text format (which we will see in the following sections), not in XML format. When used with WordFreak (see Chapter 2), output is in WordFreak XML format. When used with UIMA (see Chapter 5), output is in XML Metadata Interchange (XMI) format.

OpenNLP's README file shows how to build and use the tools. You can pipe output from one OpenNLP tool into the next, for example from the sentence detector into the tokenizer, and from the tokenizer into the POS tagger.

STANFORD NLP TOOLS
The Stanford NLP Group (`http://nlp.stanford.edu`) has also developed a set of statistical NLP tools including a POS tagger, a syntactic parser and a named entity recognizer. Like the OpenNLP tools, the Stanford NLP tools are written in Java and are mainly based on maximum entropy models. There is a difference in approach: the OpenNLP tools are designed for easy interconnection and for use as plugins in other frameworks, whereas the Stanford tagger, parser and NE recognizer are designed primarily for use as stand-alone tools.

One of the aims of the Stanford NLP Group has been to identify specific language processing phenomena where the existing accuracy levels of maximum entropy models can be improved. This can only be done by painstaking training and testing with rigorous evaluation.

3.3   SENTENCES AND TOKENIZATION

Sentence boundary detection and tokenization were introduced in Sections 2.3 and 2.4. The statistical approach to sentence boundary detection is to treat it as a classification problem. First, potential sentence boundary markers (full stops, question marks, exclamation marks) are identified. Second, they are classified into two classes: those that are sentence boundaries and those that are not.

OPENNLP SENTENCE DETECTOR

Reynar and Ratnaparkhi (1997) describe the application of maximum entropy models to sentence boundary detection as a classification task. The OpenNLP sentence detector is based on this approach.

One obvious drawback in the classification approach is that it cannot identify sentence boundaries where there is no marker. In the sonnet example, the boundary between the heading and the first line of the sonnet is not marked by a full stop, so the words of the heading are wrongly included at the beginning of the first sentence.

PRACTICAL WORK: SENTENCES AND TOKENIZATION

1. The shell script shown in Figure 3.1 runs the OpenNLP sentence detector and OpenNLP tokenizer. Change the value of OPENNLP_HOME to the name of the directory where you installed OpenNLP. Make the script executable (chmod +x opennlp-tokenizer.sh). The script takes input from stdin and sends output to stdout.

2. Use it like this to tokenize Sonnet 130:
   ./opennlp-tokenizer.sh <sonnet130.txt >tokenized130.txt &.

```
#!/bin/sh
# Shell script to run OpenNLP-1.3.0 sentence detector and tokenizer
# G. Wilcock 21.11.2007
#
# Usage: opennlp-tokenizer.sh <input.txt >tokenized.txt

OPENNLP_HOME=~gwilcock/Tools/opennlp-1.3.0
export OPENNLP_HOME

CLASSPATH=.:\
$OPENNLP_HOME/lib/opennlp-tools-1.3.0.jar:\
$OPENNLP_HOME/lib/maxent-2.4.0.jar:\
$OPENNLP_HOME/lib/trove.jar
export CLASSPATH

java opennlp.tools.lang.english.SentenceDetector \
  $OPENNLP_HOME/models/english/sentdetect/EnglishSD.bin.gz |
java opennlp.tools.lang.english.Tokenizer \
  $OPENNLP_HOME/models/english/tokenize/EnglishTok.bin.gz
```

Figure 3.1: opennlp-tokenizer.sh: A shell script to run OpenNLP sentence detector and tokenizer.

3.4   STATISTICAL TAGGING

Part-of-speech tagging was introduced in Section 2.5. The statistical approach to tagging is to treat it as a multi-way classification problem.

OPENNLP POS TAGGER

Ratnaparkhi (1996) describes the application of maximum entropy models to part-of-speech tagging. The OpenNLP POS tagger is based on this work.

PRACTICAL WORK: STATISTICAL TAGGING WITH OPENNLP TAGGER

1. The shell script shown in Figure 3.2 runs the OpenNLP POS tagger. The input is piped through OpenNLP sentence detector, OpenNLP tokenizer and OpenNLP POS tagger. Change OPENNLP_HOME to the directory where you installed OpenNLP and make the script executable (`chmod +x opennlp-tagger.sh`). The script takes input from stdin and sends output to stdout.

2. Use it like this to tag Sonnet 130:
   ```
   ./opennlp-tagger.sh <sonnet130.txt >tagged130.txt &
   ```

STANFORD POS TAGGER

After the OpenNLP tagger was developed, Toutanova and Manning (2000) and Toutanova et al. (2003) worked on improving the accuracy of maximum entropy taggers. The Stanford POS tagger (`http://nlp.stanford.edu/software/tagger.shtml`) is based on this later work.

PRACTICAL WORK: STATISTICAL TAGGING WITH STANFORD TAGGER

1. The shell script shown in Figure 3.3 runs the Stanford POS tagger. Change STANFORD_TAGGER to the name of the directory where you installed the tagger. Make the script executable (`chmod +x stanford-tagger.sh`). The script takes input from a file and sends output to stdout.

2. Use it like this to tag Sonnet 130:
   ```
   ./stanford-tagger.sh -file sonnet130.txt >tagged130.txt &
   ```

3. Note that with the OpenNLP tools, the sentence detector is run first, and its output is piped into the tokenizer. The output from the tokenizer is then piped into the OpenNLP POS tagger.

4. This is not the case with the Stanford tools. The Stanford POS tagger takes the original text as input and does its own sentence detection and tokenization.

PRACTICAL WORK: COMPARING TAGGERS

1. OpenNLP POS tagger and Stanford POS tagger produce output in a simple plain text format. The output from tagging Sonnet 130 with OpenNLP tagger is shown in Figure 3.4.

2. OpenNLP POS tagger and Stanford POS tagger both use the same Penn Treebank tagset. Compare the results of tagging Sonnet 130 with the two taggers. Which words are tagged differently? Which tagger is more accurate?

```
#!/bin/sh
# Shell script to run OpenNLP-1.3.0 POS tagger
# G. Wilcock 21.11.2007
#
# Usage: opennlp-tagger.sh <input.txt >tagged.txt

OPENNLP_HOME=~gwilcock/Tools/opennlp-1.3.0
export OPENNLP_HOME

CLASSPATH=.:\
$OPENNLP_HOME/lib/opennlp-tools-1.3.0.jar:\
$OPENNLP_HOME/lib/maxent-2.4.0.jar:\
$OPENNLP_HOME/lib/trove.jar
export CLASSPATH

java opennlp.tools.lang.english.SentenceDetector \
  $OPENNLP_HOME/models/english/sentdetect/EnglishSD.bin.gz |
java opennlp.tools.lang.english.Tokenizer \
  $OPENNLP_HOME/models/english/tokenize/EnglishTok.bin.gz |
java opennlp.tools.lang.english.PosTagger -d \
  $OPENNLP_HOME/models/english/parser/tagdict \
  $OPENNLP_HOME/models/english/parser/tag.bin.gz
```

Figure 3.2: `opennlp-tagger.sh`: A script to run OpenNLP POS tagger.

3. Tag bigger texts. Download public domain texts from Project Gutenberg (http://www.gutenberg.org), for example all 154 of Shakespeare's Sonnets, or Jane Austen's *Northanger Abbey*. Tag the texts with both OpenNLP tagger and Stanford tagger. Which tagger is faster?

3.5   CHUNKING AND PARSING

Syntactic parsing was introduced in Section 2.6. Chunking, which is also called partial parsing or shallow parsing, is quite different from full syntactic parsing. Full parsing builds syntactic structure trees of any required complexity and depth according to a comprehensive grammatical model of the language. Chunking creates very shallow trees representing simple, flat phrase structures (mainly noun phrases).

The basic approach in chunking is to exploit the work already done by the POS tagger in order to identify simple phrases by recognizing sequences of POS tags. For example, the sequence <DT, JJ, NN> (determiner, adjective, noun) can be recognized as a noun phrase (NP).

The aim of chunking is quite different from the aim of full parsing. Syntactic parsing is based on a tradition of rule-based grammars and grammar-based linguistic theories, and the aim is to capture as

```
#!/bin/sh
# Shell script to run Stanford POS tagger
# G. Wilcock 21.11.2007
#
# Usage: stanford-tagger.sh -file input.txt >tagged.txt

STANFORD_TAGGER=~gwilcock/Tools/postagger-2006-05-21
export STANFORD_TAGGER

java -Xmx300m \
  -classpath $STANFORD_TAGGER/postagger-2006-05-21.jar \
  edu.stanford.nlp.tagger.maxent.MaxentTagger \
  -model $STANFORD_TAGGER/wsj3t0-18-bidirectional/train-wsj-0-18 \
  $*
```

Figure 3.3: `stanford-tagger.sh`: A script to run Stanford POS tagger.

much as possible of the full complexity of a sentence with all its linguistic features (heads and dependents, subjects and complements, modifiers, agreement, etc.). By contrast, the aim of chunking is to support named entity recognition, as part of the practical task of information extraction from text. Chunking assists named entity recognition by identifying NPs that are candidate named entities.

OPENNLP CHUNKER
The OpenNLP tools include a chunker, which uses a maximum entropy model to recognize patterns in the POS tags made by the OpenNLP tagger. There is no Stanford chunker.

PRACTICAL WORK: CHUNKING WITH OPENNLP
1. The shell script shown in Figure 3.5 runs the OpenNLP phrase chunker. The input is piped through the OpenNLP sentence detector, tokenizer and POS tagger. Change OPENNLP_HOME to the directory where you installed OpenNLP and make the script executable. The script takes input from stdin and sends output to stdout.

2. Use it like this to do phrase chunking for Sonnet 130:
   `./opennlp-chunker.sh <sonnet130.txt >sonnet130-chunks.txt &`.

3. Try chunking bigger texts, for example all 154 Sonnets, or *Northanger Abbey*.

OPENNLP PARSER
The OpenNLP syntactic parser uses the Penn Treebank constituent tagset, which was described in Section 2.6. In contrast to the chunker, which looks for patterns in the POS tags already decided by the OpenNLP tagger, the syntactic parser takes the tokenized text as its input and makes its own part-of-speech tagging decisions.

```
Sonnet/NNP 130/CD by/IN William/NNP Shakespeare/NNP (/-LRB-
 1564-1616/CD )/-RRB-
My/PRP$ mistress/NN '/POS eyes/NNS are/VBP nothing/NN like/IN
 the/DT sun/NN ,/, Coral/NNP is/VBZ far/RB more/RBR red/JJ
 than/IN her/PRP$ lips/NNS red/JJ ./.
If/IN snow/NN be/VB white/JJ ,/, why/WRB then/RB her/PRP$
 breasts/NNS are/VBP dun/VBN ,/, If/IN hairs/NNS be/VB wires/NNS
 ,/, black/JJ wires/NNS grow/VB on/IN her/PRP$ head/NN ./.
I/PRP have/VBP seen/VBN roses/NNS damasked/VBD ,/, red/JJ and/CC
 white/JJ ,/, But/CC no/DT such/JJ roses/NNS see/VBP I/PRP in/RB
 her/PRP$ cheeks/NNS ./.
And/CC in/IN some/DT perfumes/NNS is/VBZ there/RB more/JJR
 delight/NN Than/IN in/IN the/DT breath/NN that/IN from/IN
 my/PRP$ mistress/NN reeks/NNS ./.
I/PRP love/VBP to/TO hear/VB her/PRP speak/VB ,/, yet/RB well/RB
 I/PRP know/VBP That/DT music/NN hath/VBZ a/DT far/RB more/RBR
 pleasing/JJ sound/NN ./.
I/PRP grant/VBP I/PRP never/RB saw/VBD a/DT goddess/NN go/VB ,/,
 My/PRP$ mistress/NN when/WRB she/PRP walks/VBZ ,/, treads/NNS
 on/IN the/DT ground/NN ./.
And/CC yet/RB ,/, by/IN Heaven/NNP ,/, I/PRP think/VBP my/PRP$
 love/NN as/IN rare/JJ As/IN any/DT she/PRP belied/VBN with/IN
 false/JJ compare/NN ./.
```

Figure 3.4:   The sonnet tagged by OpenNLP POS tagger.

PRACTICAL WORK: STATISTICAL PARSING WITH OPENNLP

1. The shell script shown in Figure 3.6 runs the OpenNLP parser. The input is piped through the OpenNLP sentence detector, OpenNLP tokenizer and OpenNLP parser. Change OPENNLP_HOME to the directory where you installed OpenNLP and make the script executable. The script takes input from stdin and sends output to stdout.

2. Use it like this to parse Sonnet 130:
   ./opennlp-parser.sh <sonnet130.txt >parsed130.txt &.

3. The result should look something like Figure 3.7.

STANFORD PARSER

The Stanford parser is actually a set of alternative parsing algorithms and statistical models (see http://nlp.stanford.edu/software/lex-parser.shtml). It was developed in order to compare and evaluate different techniques.

```
#!/bin/sh
# Shell script to run OpenNLP-1.3.0 chunker
# G. Wilcock 21.11.2007
#
# Usage: ./opennlp-chunker.sh < input.txt > chunked.txt

OPENNLP_HOME=~gwilcock/Tools/opennlp-1.3.0
export OPENNLP_HOME

CLASSPATH=.:\
$OPENNLP_HOME/lib/opennlp-tools-1.3.0.jar:\
$OPENNLP_HOME/lib/maxent-2.4.0.jar:\
$OPENNLP_HOME/lib/trove.jar
export CLASSPATH

java opennlp.tools.lang.english.SentenceDetector \
  $OPENNLP_HOME/models/english/sentdetect/EnglishSD.bin.gz |
java opennlp.tools.lang.english.Tokenizer \
  $OPENNLP_HOME/models/english/tokenize/EnglishTok.bin.gz |
java opennlp.tools.lang.english.PosTagger -d \
  $OPENNLP_HOME/models/english/parser/tagdict \
  $OPENNLP_HOME/models/english/parser/tag.bin.gz |
java opennlp.tools.lang.english.TreebankChunker \
  $OPENNLP_HOME/models/english/chunker/EnglishChunk.bin.gz
```

Figure 3.5: opennlp-chunker.sh: A script to run OpenNLP chunker.

Parsing with unlexicalized probabilistic context-free grammars (PCFGs) is described by (Klein and Manning 2003a). Statistical parsing with lexicalized grammars is described by (Klein and Manning 2003b).

PRACTICAL WORK: STATISTICAL PARSING WITH STANFORD PARSER

1. The shell script shown in Figure 3.8 runs the Stanford statistical parser. Change STAN-FORD_PARSER to the directory where you installed the parser and make the script executable. The script takes input from a file and sends output to stdout.

2. Use it like this to parse Sonnet 130:
   ```
   ./stanford-parser.sh -file sonnet130.txt >parsed130.txt &.
   ```

3. Note that the Stanford parser takes the original text as input and does its own sentence detection and tokenization. This differs from the OpenNLP parser, whose input is piped from the OpenNLP sentence detector and the OpenNLP tokenizer.

4. The script in Figure 3.9 runs the same parser and the same grammar with a graphical user interface. Change STANFORD_PARSER to the directory where you installed the parser and make the script executable.

5. Figure 3.10 shows the Stanford parser GUI when parsing Sonnet 130.

PRACTICAL WORK: COMPARING TAGGERS AND PARSERS

1. Use the OpenNLP tagger to do automatic POS tagging of *Northanger Abbey* and save the results. Approximately how long does it take?

2. Use the OpenNLP parser to do automatic syntactic parsing of *Northanger Abbey* and save the results. Approximately how long does it take?

3. The parser output includes POS tags on individual words as well as constituent labels on syntactic constituents. Look at the tags in the parser output and in the tagger output. Does the parser have the same tags, or does it do its own tagging?

4. Can you design a systematic method to compare POS tags in the parser output and in the tagger output? For example, what percentage of the tags are the same?

```
#!/bin/sh
# Shell script to run OpenNLP-1.3.0 parser
# G. Wilcock 21.11.2007
#
# Usage: opennlp-parser.sh <input.txt >parsed.txt

OPENNLP_HOME=~gwilcock/Tools/opennlp-1.3.0
export OPENNLP_HOME

CLASSPATH=.:\
$OPENNLP_HOME/lib/opennlp-tools-1.3.0.jar:\
$OPENNLP_HOME/lib/maxent-2.4.0.jar:\
$OPENNLP_HOME/lib/trove.jar
export CLASSPATH

java opennlp.tools.lang.english.SentenceDetector \
  $OPENNLP_HOME/models/english/sentdetect/EnglishSD.bin.gz |
java opennlp.tools.lang.english.Tokenizer \
  $OPENNLP_HOME/models/english/tokenize/EnglishTok.bin.gz |
java -Xmx1024m opennlp.tools.lang.english.TreebankParser -d \
  $OPENNLP_HOME/models/english/parser
```

Figure 3.6: `opennlp-parser.sh`: A script to run OpenNLP parser.

```
(TOP (NP (NNP Sonnet) (CD 130)))
(TOP (PP (IN by) (NP (NP (NNP William) (NNP Shakespeare))
  (PRN (-LRB- -LRB-) (NP (CD 1564-1616)) (-RRB- -RRB-)))))
(TOP (S (S (NP (NP (PRP$ My) (NN mistress) (POS ')) (NNS eyes))
 (VP (VBP are) (NP (NP (NN nothing))
 (PP (IN like) (NP (DT the) (NN sun)))))) (, ,)
 (NP (NNP Coral)) (VP (VBZ is)
 (ADJP (ADJP (ADVP (RB far) (RBR more)) (JJ red))
 (PP (IN than) (NP (NP (PRP$ her) (NNS lips)) (ADJP (JJ red)))))) (. .)))
(TOP (SBARQ (SBAR (IN If)
 (S (NP (NN snow)) (VP (VB be) (ADJP (JJ white))))) (, ,)
 (WHADVP (WRB why)) (SQ (SBAR (RB then)
 (S (S (NP (PRP$ her) (NNS breasts)) (VP (VBP are) (VP (VBN dun)))) (, ,)
 (S (SBAR (IN If) (S (NP (NNS hairs)) (VP (VB be) (NP (NNS wires))))) (, ,)
 (NP (JJ black) (NNS wires))
 (VP (VBP grow) (PP (IN on) (NP (PRP$ her) (NN head))))))))) (. .)))
(TOP (S (S (NP (PRP I)) (VP (VBP have) (VP (VBN seen) (NP (NP (NP (NNS roses))
 (VP (VBD damasked))) (, ,) (ADJP (JJ red) (CC and) (JJ white)))))) (, ,)
 (CC But) (S (NP (DT no) (JJ such) (NNS roses))
 (VP (VBP see) (NP (NP (PRP I))
 (PP (IN in) (NP (PRP$ her) (NNS cheeks)))))) (. .)))
(TOP (S (CC And) (PP (IN in) (NP (DT some) (NNS perfumes)))
 (VP (VBZ is) (NP (NP (RB there) (JJR more) (NN delight)
 (NNP Than)) (PP (IN in) (NP (DT the) (NN breath)))
 (PP (IN that) (PP (IN from) (NP (PRP$ my) (NN mistress) (NNS reeks))))))
 (. .)))
(TOP (S (S (NP (PRP I)) (VP (VBP love)
 (S (VP (TO to) (VP (VB hear) (S (NP (PRP her)) (VP (VB speak)))))))) (, ,)
 (S (ADVP (RB yet) (RB well)) (NP (PRP I)) (VP (VBP know)
 (SBAR (S (NP (DT That) (NN music)) (VP (VBZ hath)
 (NP (DT a) (ADJP (ADVP (RB far) (RBR more)) (JJ pleasing)) (NN sound)))))))
 (. .)))
(TOP (S (NP (PRP I)) (VP (VBP grant) (SBAR (S (NP (PRP I)) (ADVP (RB never))
 (VP (VBD saw) (NP (NP (DT a) (JJ goddess) (NN go)) (, ,)
 (NP (NP (NP (PRP$ My) (NN mistress))
 (SBAR (WHADVP (WRB when)) (S (NP (PRP she)) (VP (VBZ walks))))) (, ,)
 (NP (NP (NNS treads)) (PP (IN on) (NP (DT the) (NN ground))))))))))) (. .)))
(TOP (S (CONJP (CC And) (RB yet)) (, ,) (PP (IN by) (NP (NNP Heaven))) (, ,)
 (NP (PRP I)) (VP (VBP think) (NP (NP (PRP$ my) (NN love))
 (PP (IN as) (NP (JJ rare))))
 (SBAR (IN As) (S (NP (DT any) (PRP she))
 (VP (VBN belied) (PP (IN with) (NP (JJ false) (NN compare)))))))) (. .)))
```

Figure 3.7: The sonnet parsed by OpenNLP parser.

```
#!/bin/sh
# Shell script to run Stanford PCFG parser
# G. Wilcock 21.11.2007
#
# Usage: stanford-parser.sh -file input.txt >parsed.txt

STANFORD_PARSER=~gwilcock/Tools/stanford-parser-2007-08-19
export STANFORD_PARSER

java -server -Xmx300m \
  -classpath $STANFORD_PARSER/stanford-parser.jar \
  edu.stanford.nlp.parser.lexparser.LexicalizedParser \
  $STANFORD_PARSER/englishPCFG.ser.gz \
  $*
```

Figure 3.8: `stanford-parser.sh`: A script to run Stanford parser.

5. Use the Stanford tagger to do automatic POS tagging of *Northanger Abbey* and save the results. Approximately how long does it take?

6. Use the Stanford parser to do automatic syntactic parsing of *Northanger Abbey* and save the results. Approximately how long does it take?

7. Does the Stanford parser have the same tags as the Stanford tagger?

8. In the Stanford case, can you use the same systematic method as in the OpenNLP case, to compare POS tags in the parser and tagger output?

9. Examine some cases where words were given different tags by the tagger and the parser. Does the parser use the additional information from its syntactic analysis to make improvements on the POS decisions made by the tagger? Or does the parser ignore good POS tagging and force the tags to fit the parse structures?

PRACTICAL WORK: COMPARING PARSERS

1. Compare the results of parsing Sonnet 130 with OpenNLP parser and with Stanford parser. (There is a brief comment in Chapter 5, Section 5.6). Which sentences and phrases are parsed differently? Which parser is more accurate?

2. Try parsing bigger texts, for example all 154 Sonnets, or *Northanger Abbey*. Which parser is faster?

3.6 NAMED ENTITY RECOGNITION

The task of named entity recognition is to identify words and phrases that mention entities of specific types. For example, *William Shakespeare* is an entity of type `Person`, and *IBM* is an entity of type `Organization`.

```sh
#!/bin/sh
# Shell script to run Stanford parser GUI
# G. Wilcock 21.11.2007
#
# Usage: ./stanford-parser-GUI.sh &

STANFORD_PARSER=~gwilcock/Tools/stanford-parser-2007-08-19
export STANFORD_PARSER

java -server -Xmx600m \
  -classpath $STANFORD_PARSER/stanford-parser.jar \
  edu.stanford.nlp.parser.ui.Parser \
  $STANFORD_PARSER/englishPCFG.ser.gz \
  $*
```

Figure 3.9: `stanford-parser-gui.sh`: A script to run Stanford parser GUI.

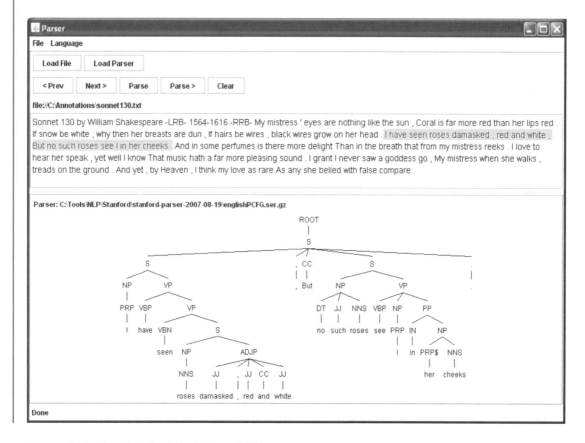

Figure 3.10: Stanford Statistical Parser GUI.

OPENNLP NAME FINDER

OpenNLP name finder uses maximum entropy models to recognize names of different types of entities: persons, locations, organizations, dates, times, money and percentages. In addition to these seven types, which have ready-made models available for download, you can create your own models to enable name finder to recognize other types of entities. This is described in Chapter 6.

PRACTICAL WORK: NAMED ENTITY RECOGNITION WITH OPENNLP

1. The shell script shown in Figure 3.11 runs the OpenNLP name finder. The input is piped through the OpenNLP sentence detector and the OpenNLP name finder. Change OPENNLP_HOME to the directory where you installed OpenNLP and make the script executable. The script takes input from stdin and sends output to stdout.

2. Use it like this to do named entity recognition for Sonnet 130:
   ./opennlp-namefinder.sh <sonnet130.txt >sonnet130-names.txt &.

3. There are not many named entities in the sonnets. Try other texts, for example *Northanger Abbey*.

```
#!/bin/sh
# Shell script to run OpenNLP-1.3.0 name finder
# using the complete set of ready-trained models
# G. Wilcock 21.11.2007
#
# Usage: ./opennlp-namefinder.sh < input.txt > namesfound.txt

OPENNLP_HOME=~gwilcock/Tools/opennlp-1.3.0
export OPENNLP_HOME

CLASSPATH=.:\
$OPENNLP_HOME/lib/opennlp-tools-1.3.0.jar:\
$OPENNLP_HOME/lib/maxent-2.4.0.jar:\
$OPENNLP_HOME/lib/trove.jar
export CLASSPATH

java opennlp.tools.lang.english.SentenceDetector \
 $OPENNLP_HOME/models/english/sentdetect/EnglishSD.bin.gz |
java -Xmx1024m opennlp.tools.lang.english.NameFinder \
 $OPENNLP_HOME/models/english/namefind/*.bin.gz
```

Figure 3.11: opennlp-namefinder.sh: A script to run OpenNLP name finder.

STANFORD NAMED ENTITY RECOGNIZER

The Stanford named entity recognizer is based on conditional random field models (`http://nlp.stanford.edu/software/CRF-NER.shtml`) as discussed in (Finkel et al. 2005). Stanford NER can optionally be used with a GUI as shown in Figure 3.12.

Figure 3.12: Stanford Named Entity Recognizer GUI.

PRACTICAL WORK: STANFORD NAMED ENTITY RECOGNIZER

1. The shell script shown in Figure 3.13 runs the Stanford Named Entity Recognizer (NER). Change STANFORD_NER to the directory where you installed Stanford NER and make the script executable. The script takes input from a file and sends output to stdout.

2. Use it like this to do named entity recognition for Sonnet 130:
   `./stanford-ner.sh sonnet130.txt >sonnet130-names.txt &`.

3. The script shown in Figure 3.14 runs the Stanford NER with a graphical user interface (GUI). Change STANFORD_NER to the directory where you installed Stanford NER and make the script executable.

4. Figure 3.12 shows the Stanford NER GUI in use.

```
#!/bin/sh
# Shell script to run Stanford NER
# G. Wilcock 21.11.2007
#
# Usage: stanford-ner.sh input.txt >names.txt

STANFORD_NER=~gwilcock/Tools/stanford-ner-2007-11-05
export STANFORD_NER

java -mx600m \
  -classpath $STANFORD_NER/stanford-ner.jar \
  edu.stanford.nlp.ie.crf.CRFClassifier \
  -loadClassifier \
   $STANFORD_NER/classifiers/ner-eng-ie.crf-3-all2006.ser.gz \
  -textFile $1
```

Figure 3.13: `stanford-ner.sh`: A script to run Stanford NER.

```
#!/bin/sh
# Shell script to run Stanford NER GUI
# G. Wilcock 21.11.2007
#
# Usage: stanford-ner-gui.sh

STANFORD_NER=~gwilcock/Tools/stanford-ner-2007-11-05
export STANFORD_NER

java -mx600m \
  -classpath $STANFORD_NER/stanford-ner.jar \
  edu.stanford.nlp.ie.crf.NERGUI
```

Figure 3.14: `stanford-ner-gui.sh`: A script to run Stanford NER GUI.

3.7 COREFERENCE RESOLUTION

Coreference was introduced in Section 2.7. Automatic coreference resolution is difficult, as it requires both linguistic knowledge and knowledge of the world.

The OpenNLP tools include a coreference linker, which uses the results of other OpenNLP tools. There is no Stanford coreference tool.

OPENNLP COREFERENCE LINKER

OpenNLP coreference linker takes advantage of the information provided by first doing syntactic parsing and named entity recognition. OpenNLP also uses information from WordNet as a substitute for knowledge of the world.

```sh
#!/bin/sh
# Shell script to run OpenNLP-1.3.0 coreference linker
# G. Wilcock 27.06.2008
#
# Usage: ./opennlp-coreference.sh < input.txt > coref.txt

OPENNLP_HOME=~gwilcock/Tools/opennlp-1.3.0
export OPENNLP_HOME


WORDNET_HOME=~gwilcock/Tools/wordnet-2.0
export WORDNET_HOME


CLASSPATH=.:\
$OPENNLP_HOME/lib/opennlp-tools-1.3.0.jar:\
$OPENNLP_HOME/lib/maxent-2.4.0.jar:\
$OPENNLP_HOME/lib/trove.jar:\
$OPENNLP_HOME/lib/jwnl-1.3.3.jar
export CLASSPATH


java opennlp.tools.lang.english.SentenceDetector \
  $OPENNLP_HOME/models/english/sentdetect/EnglishSD.bin.gz |
java opennlp.tools.lang.english.Tokenizer \
  $OPENNLP_HOME/models/english/tokenize/EnglishTok.bin.gz |
java -Xmx1024m opennlp.tools.lang.english.TreebankParser -d \
  $OPENNLP_HOME/models/english/parser |
java -Xmx1024m opennlp.tools.lang.english.NameFinder -parse \
  $OPENNLP_HOME/models/english/namefind/*.bin.gz |
java -Xmx1024m -DWNSEARCHDIR=$WORDNET_HOME/dict -Duser.language=en \
  opennlp.tools.lang.english.TreebankLinker \
  $OPENNLP_HOME/models/english/coref
```

Figure 3.15: `opennlp-coreference.sh`: A script to run OpenNLP coreference.

PRACTICAL WORK: COREFERENCE WITH OPENNLP

1. The shell script shown in Figure 3.15 runs the OpenNLP coreference linker. The input is piped through the OpenNLP sentence detector, tokenizer, parser, name finder and coreference linker. Change the values of OPENNLP_HOME and WORDNET_HOME to the correct locations and make the script executable. The script takes input from stdin and sends output to stdout.

2. Use it like this to do coreference for Sonnet 130:
   ```
   ./opennlp-coreference.sh <sonnet130.txt >sonnet130-coref.txt &
   ```

3. The result should look something like Figure 3.16.

Some of the coreference links in Figure 3.16 are correct and some are incorrect. The initial NP *My mistress* is annotated as NP#25, and the possessive pronoun *her* in *her lips* is annotated NML#25, correctly showing that these two entities are coreferents. Similarly, *her* in *her breasts* and *her* in *her head* are both annotated NML#25, correctly showing that they are also coreferents of *My mistress*. However, *her* in *her cheeks* is annotated NML#20, incorrectly making a coreference with *snow*.

The personal pronoun *I* in *I have seen roses...* is annotated NP#22, and *I* in *no such roses see I...* is also NP#22, correctly showing that they corefer. However, *her* in *hear her speak* is annotated NP#2, incorrectly making a coreference with *I* in *I love to hear....*

The personal pronoun *I* in *I grant...* is annotated NP#9, and *I* in *I never saw...* is also NP#9, correctly showing that they corefer. The possessive pronoun *My* in the following *My mistress* is also correctly annotated NML#9, a third coreference with *I*. The final *any she* is correctly parsed as a noun phrase, and is correctly annotated NP#2 as a coreference with *she* in *she walks*.

3.8   FURTHER READING

- The standard textbook on statistical NLP is (Manning and Schütze 1999).

- Statistical tagging: See (Manning and Schütze 1999) Chapter 10 and (Jurafsky and Martin 2008) Chapter 5.

- Statistical parsing: See (Manning and Schütze 1999) Chapters 11 and 12 and (Jurafsky and Martin 2008) Chapter 14.

- Maximum entropy models: See (Manning and Schütze 1999) Chapter 16.2.

```
(TOP (NP (NNP Sonnet) (CD 130)) )
(TOP (PP (IN by) (NP (person (NP (NNP William) (NNP Shakespeare))
 (PRN (-LRB- -LRB-) (NP (CD 1564-1616)) (-RRB- -RRB-)))))) )
(TOP (S (S (NP (NP#25 (NML (PRP$ My)) (NN mistress) (POS ')) (NNS eyes))
 (VP (VBP are) (NP (NP (NN nothing))
 (PP (IN like) (NP (DT the) (NN sun)))))) (, ,)
 (NP (NNP Coral)) (VP (VBZ is)
 (ADJP (ADJP (ADVP (RB far) (RBR more)) (JJ red))
 (PP (IN than) (NP (NP (NML#25 (PRP$ her)) (NNS lips)) (ADJP (JJ red))))))
 (. .)) )
(TOP (SBARQ (SBAR (IN If)
 (S (NP#20 (NN snow)) (VP (VB be) (ADJP (JJ white)))))) (, ,)
 (WHADVP (WRB why)) (SQ (SBAR (RB then) (S (S (NP (NML#25 (PRP$ her))
 (NNS breasts)) (VP (VBP are) (VP (VBN dun)))) (, ,)
 (S (SBAR (IN If) (S (NP (NNS hairs)) (VP (VB be) (NP (NNS wires))))) (, ,)
 (NP (JJ black) (NNS wires)) (VP (VBP grow)
 (PP (IN on) (NP (NML#25 (PRP$ her)) (NN head)))))))) (. .)) )
(TOP (S (S (NP#22 (PRP I)) (VP (VBP have) (VP (VBN seen)
 (NP (NP (NP (NNS roses)) (VP (VBD damasked))) (, ,)
 (ADJP (JJ red) (CC and) (JJ white)))))) (, ,)
 (CC But) (S (NP (DT no) (JJ such) (NNS roses))
 (VP (VBP see) (NP#22 (NP (PRP I))
 (PP (IN in) (NP (NML#20 (PRP$ her)) (NNS cheeks)))))) (. .)) )
(TOP (S (CC And) (PP (IN in) (NP (DT some) (NNS perfumes)))
 (VP (VBZ is) (NP (NP (RB there) (JJR more) (NN delight)
 (NNP Than)) (PP (IN in) (NP (DT the) (NN breath))) (PP (IN that)
 (PP (IN from) (NP (NML (PRP$ my)) (NN mistress) (NNS reeks))))))
 (. .)) )
(TOP (S (S (NP#2 (PRP I)) (VP (VBP love) (S (VP (TO to)
 (VP (VB hear) (S (NP#2 (PRP her)) (VP (VB speak))))))))) (, ,)
 (S (ADVP (RB yet) (RB well)) (NP (PRP I)) (VP (VBP know)
 (SBAR (S (NP (DT That) (NN music)) (VP (VBZ hath)
 (NP (DT a) (ADJP (ADVP (RB far) (RBR more)) (JJ pleasing)) (NN sound)))))))
 (. .)) )
(TOP (S (NP#9 (PRP I)) (VP (VBP grant) (SBAR (S (NP#9 (PRP I))
 (ADVP (RB never)) (VP (VBD saw) (NP (NP (DT a) (JJ goddess) (NN go)) (, ,)
 (NP (NP (NP (NML#9 (PRP$ My)) (NN mistress))
 (SBAR (WHADVP (WRB when)) (S (NP#2 (PRP she)) (VP (VBZ walks))))) (, ,)
 (NP (NP (NNS treads)) (PP (IN on) (NP (DT the) (NN ground)))))))))
 (. .)) )
(TOP (S (CONJP (CC And) (RB yet)) (, ,) (PP (IN by) (NP (NNP Heaven))) (, ,)
 (NP (PRP I)) (VP (VBP think) (NP (NP (NML (PRP$ my)) (NN love))
 (PP (IN as) (NP (JJ rare))))
 (SBAR (IN As) (S (NP#2 (DT any) (PRP she))
 (VP (VBN belied) (PP (IN with) (NP (JJ false) (NN compare))))))))) (. .)) )
```

Figure 3.16:   The sonnet with OpenNLP coreference annotations.

C H A P T E R   4

Annotation Interchange

In Chapter 1, we claimed that one of the advantages of XML is that it supports the interchange of annotations because we can transform annotations from one XML format to another. This allows the results of one annotation tool to be used by another tool that works with a different format. In this chapter, we demonstrate the truth of this claim by showing specific examples of XSLT transformations between different formats.

4.1   XSLT TRANSFORMATIONS

A thorough guide to XSLT transformations is provided by Doug Tidwell in his book *XSLT: Mastering XML Transformations* (Tidwell 2001). He shows how to write XSLT stylesheets that perform a wide range of transformations, including methods for removing, inserting, renaming, and reordering XML elements and their attributes. He shows how to produce HTML, XML and plain text outputs. In Chapter 1, we used one of Tidwell's example stylesheets to transform Sonnet 130 from XML to HTML. In this chapter, we describe more advanced XSLT transformations that can be applied to linguistic annotations.

XSLT can be used for XML-to-XML transformations. In Chapter 2, we saw examples of the stand-off XML annotation format produced by WordFreak. Here, we show how to transform the WordFreak XML format so that it includes the words of the text, not merely their start and end points. This requires a method for reading in the text as a secondary input file to the XSLT processor. We see how to do this in this section.

XSLT can also be used for XML-to-non-XML transformations. In Chapter 3, we saw that OpenNLP tools produce annotations in a simple non-XML plain text format. We show how to transform WordFreak XML format into OpenNLP plain text format in Section 4.2.

XSLT can even be used for non-XML-to-XML transformations, with some Java code to do the initial input processing. We refer the reader to Chapter 5 of Eric Burke's excellent book *Java and XSLT* (Burke 2001).

We used GATE in Chapter 1 to illustrate the idea of stand-off annotations. Details of the GATE XML format are described in Section 4.3. We show how to transform GATE XML format to WordFreak XML format in Section 4.4.

XML Metadata Interchange (XMI) is an interchange format that has been proposed as a standard to support the interchange of annotations produced by different tools. Although XMI has not yet been widely adopted, it is used by the UIMA architecture described in Chapter 5. We describe the XMI format in Section 4.5. As an example of transforming other formats to XMI, Section 4.6 shows how to transform WordFreak XML format to XMI format.

ADDING THE WORDS TO WORDFREAK
Our first example of a more advanced XSLT stylesheet is an XML-to-XML transformation. We saw in Chapter 2 that the WordFreak annotation file does not include the words of the annotated text. Instead, it has a `span` attribute that points to the start and end of each word in the original text. This is how the first word of Sonnet 130 (the possessive pronoun *My*) is annotated in this format:

```
<Annotation type="PRP$" span="63..65"
  confidence="0.9567615294617327" annotator="tagger" id="13"/>
```

We now describe an XSLT stylesheet that takes a WordFreak annotation file and transforms it into a modified format that includes the words of the original text. The same example after the transformation:

```
<Annotation type="PRP$" word="My" span="63..65"
  confidence="0.9567615294617327" annotator="tagger" id="13"/>
```

To get the correct words for the sonnet, the stylesheet needs to read a second file, containing the sonnet text that was annotated. XSLT stylesheets can read external XML documents using the `document()` function. However, the document to be read must be in XML format. So we must put the sonnet text into an XML file. For a minimal XML format, we put `<text>` at the start and `</text>` at the end. We add an XML header just to be clear that this is an XML file. The resulting file, `sonnet130.text.xml`, is shown in Figure 4.1.

```
<?xml version="1.0"?>
<text>
             Sonnet 130


by William Shakespeare (1564-1616)



My mistress' eyes are nothing like the sun,
Coral is far more red than her lips red.
If snow be white, why then her breasts are dun,
If hairs be wires, black wires grow on her head.
I have seen roses damasked, red and white,
But no such roses see I in her cheeks.
And in some perfumes is there more delight
Than in the breath that from my mistress reeks.
I love to hear her speak, yet well I know
That music hath a far more pleasing sound.
I grant I never saw a goddess go,
My mistress when she walks, treads on the ground.
And yet, by Heaven, I think my love as rare
As any she belied with false compare.
</text>
```

Figure 4.1: `sonnet130.text.xml`: The sonnet text as an XML file.

It is essential that the text in the file is an exact copy of the original text that was annotated. It must not be edited in any way, because the "spans" in the sonnet annotation file must match the words in the sonnet text file exactly.

GLOBAL PARAMETERS AND GLOBAL VARIABLES

The stylesheet `wf2wfplus.xsl` for this transformation is shown in Figures 4.2 to 4.3. The stylesheet reads information from the existing WordFreak annotation file and writes information to a new modified XML annotation file. The beginning of the stylesheet (Figure 4.2) specifies that the output file will be in XML format by `<xsl:output method="xml"/>`.

```
<xsl:stylesheet version="1.0"
  xmlns:xsl="http://www.w3.org/1999/XSL/Transform">
  <xsl:output method="xml"/>
  <!-- Global parameter for text file name -->
  <xsl:param name="textfile"/>

  <!-- Global variable for newline -->
  <xsl:variable name="newline">
    <xsl:text>
</xsl:text>
  </xsl:variable>

  <xsl:template match="/">
    <xsl:apply-templates select="AnnotationFile"/>
  </xsl:template>

  <xsl:template match="AnnotationFile">
    <xsl:value-of select="$newline"/>
    <xsl:element name="AnnotationFile">
      <!-- Copy all attributes -->
      <xsl:copy-of select="@*" />
      <xsl:value-of select="$newline"/>
      <!-- Process nested annotations -->
      <xsl:apply-templates select="*"/>
    </xsl:element>
    <xsl:value-of select="$newline"/>
  </xsl:template>
```

Figure 4.2: `wf2wfplus.xsl`: Adding the words to WordFreak (1).

In this example, the text file contains the text of `sonnet130.txt`, but it's best to make a general stylesheet that can be used with any text. The name of the text file is therefore supplied to the stylesheet as a parameter. The stylesheet creates a global parameter in Figure 4.2 by `<xsl:param name="textfile">`.

It's good to insert newlines into the output file at certain places in order to improve its readability, especially while developing a new stylesheet. A convenient way to do this in XSLT is to create a global

```
<xsl:template match="features|annotators">
  <!-- Copy entire element -->
  <xsl:copy-of select="."/>
  <xsl:value-of select="$newline"/>
</xsl:template>

<xsl:template match="Annotation[@type='file' or @type='sentence']">
  <xsl:element name="Annotation">
    <!-- Copy all attributes -->
    <xsl:copy-of select="@*" />
    <xsl:value-of select="$newline"/>
    <!-- Process nested annotations -->
    <xsl:apply-templates select="*"/>
  </xsl:element>
  <xsl:value-of select="$newline"/>
</xsl:template>

<xsl:template match="Annotation">
  <!-- Get start (x) and end (y) from span="x..y" attribute -->
  <xsl:variable name="x" select="substring-before(@span,'..')"/>
  <xsl:variable name="y" select="substring-after(@span,'..')"/>
  <xsl:element name="Annotation">
    <!-- Keep type as first attribute -->
    <xsl:copy-of select="@type" />
    <!-- Insert word as second attribute -->
    <xsl:attribute name="word">
      <xsl:value-of select="substring(document($textfile),
                                      $x+1, $y - $x)"/>
    </xsl:attribute>
    <!-- Copy remaining attributes -->
    <xsl:copy-of select="@*" />
  </xsl:element>
  <xsl:value-of select="$newline"/>
</xsl:template>

<!-- Ignore anything else -->
<xsl:template match="*|@*|text()"/>
</xsl:stylesheet>
```

Figure 4.3: `wf2wfplus.xsl`: Adding the words to WordFreak (2).

variable with a newline as its value. The global variable is created in Figure 4.2 by `<xsl:variable name="newline">`. The value of the variable is set to newline by `<xsl:text>` followed by a newline followed by `</xsl:text>`. Whenever a newline is to be inserted into the output, this can then be done simply by `<xsl:value-of select="$newline"/>`, as seen in the template at the end of Figure 4.2.

COPYING ELEMENTS AND ATTRIBUTES

The output file will have new information about the words, but it must also include all the information from the existing file. None of the existing information must be lost, it must be carefully copied from the input file.

A complete element can be copied from the input file to the output file by `<xsl:copy-of>`. This is fine for the elements that do not need to be changed, for example the `<annotators>` and `<features>` elements. In the second part of the stylesheet (Figure 4.3), these elements are matched by `<xsl:template match="features|annotators">` and their entire contents copied to the output file by `<xsl:copy-of select="."/>`. Note that `<xsl:copy>` copies an element without its attributes, `<xsl:copy-of>` copies it with its attributes.

Most of the `<Annotation>` elements need to be changed in order to add a new "word" attribute. This can be done by making new versions of the input elements in the output file, using `<xsl:element>`. To make new `<Annotation>` elements, `<xsl:element name="Annotation">` is used.

When necessary, existing attributes can be copied into the new elements one by one. For example, the existing type attribute is copied by `<xsl:copy-of select="@type">`. When all input attributes need to be copied, this is more conveniently done by `<xsl:copy-of select="@*">`.

GETTING THE WORDS OF THE ORIGINAL TEXT

New attributes can be added to the output elements by `<xsl:attribute>`. The purpose of this stylesheet is to add a new word attribute. This is easily created by `<xsl:attribute name="word">`. Getting the correct string value for the word is a little more complicated.

In order to get access to the words for the sonnet, the stylesheet reads a second file containing the original text that was annotated, using the `document()` function. Here, the stylesheet receives the name of the file containing the text as a global parameter (`<xsl:param name="textfile">` in Figure 4.2). The value of the parameter is passed to the `document()` function by `document($textfile)`.

In order to extract individual words from the text, the stylesheet uses XPath functions for strings. The `substring(text, start, length)` function is used to get substrings from a text. The parameters are the text, the substring start position (starting from 1, not 0), and the substring length.

The start position and length for each word are calculated using the numbers given in its span attribute in the form `span="x..y"`. Basically, x is the start and y is the end, so the length is `y - x`. However, care must be taken with the numbers. In the span attribute x starts from 0, but x+1 is needed for the substring start position (which starts from 1, not 0).

It is convenient to declare x and y as local variables in the template that does the calculation (`<xsl:variable name="x">` and `<xsl:variable name="y">` in Figure 4.3). To extract the x and y values from the `span="x..y"` attribute, the stylesheet uses the XPath functions `substring-before(@span,'..')` to get the x value and `substring-after(@span,'..')` to get the y value.

PRACTICAL WORK: ADDING WORDS TO THE WORDFREAK FORMAT

1. Add the words of the sonnet to the WordFreak XML format using the stylesheet `wf2wfplus.xsl` shown in Figures 4.2 to 4.3, together with the text file `sonnet130.text.xml` shown in Figure 4.1.

2. The normal WordFreak annotations file is the input file, and the name of the sonnet text file is given as a parameter. If you use the xalan.sh script, this is done as follows:
   ```
   ./xalan.sh -in sonnet130.txt.ann -xsl wf2wfplus.xsl
   -out sonnet130.wfplus.ann -param textfile sonnet130.text.xml.
   ```

4.2   WORDFREAK-OPENNLP TRANSFORMATION

.

In Chapter 2, we used OpenNLP tools as WordFreak plugins, producing annotations in WordFreak XML format, and in Chapter 3, we used OpenNLP tools by themselves, producing annotations in a simple non-XML plain text format. It is useful to be able to interchange annotations between these formats. We will describe an XSLT stylesheet that transforms WordFreak XML format into OpenNLP plain text format. We do not provide a stylesheet to transform OpenNLP format to WordFreak format, as the OpenNLP tools can be run inside WordFreak to produce WordFreak XML format.

EDITING OPENNLP TAGS IN WORDFREAK

The statistical tagging done by the OpenNLP POS tagger inevitably contains errors, especially when the text includes older words or unusual word order in poetry. For example, in the sonnet the word *dun* was tagged VBN, as shown in OpenNLP format in Chapter 3 (Figure 3.4) and in WordFreak in Figure 4.4. In fact, *dun* is an adjective meaning brown or dusky, contrasting with *white* in the sonnet, so the correct category is JJ (adjective). Another incorrectly-tagged word is *there*, which should be EX (existential). Two other clear errors are *reeks* and *treads*, which are tagged NNS (noun plural) but should be VBZ (verb present tense third person singular).

The WordFreak graphical interface can be conveniently used to edit incorrect tags. After running the OpenNLP POS tagger in WordFreak, *dun* is incorrectly tagged VBN (Figure 4.4). The annotator is "tagger", an automatic annotator. After clicking on JJ in the WordFreak POS tag menu, *dun* is correctly tagged JJ (Figure 4.5). The annotator is now "gw", a human annotator.

TRANSFORMING WORDFREAK XML TO OPENNLP PLAIN TEXT

We now describe the stylesheet that transforms WordFreak XML format into OpenNLP plain text format. This example handles annotations for sentence boundaries, tokens and POS tags, but does not handle syntactic constituents or named entities. The stylesheet `wf2open.xsl` is shown in Figures 4.6 and 4.7.

The stylesheet reads WordFreak annotations as before, so the input processing is similar to the previous stylesheet, but the output is quite different as the annotations are written to a plain text file in OpenNLP format. The beginning of the stylesheet (Figure 4.6) specifies that the output file will be in text format by `<xsl:output method="text"/>`.

As the OpenNLP format includes the words of the text, the stylesheet must get the words from a separate text file. This is done in the same way as `wf2wfplus.xsl` in Section 4.1. The declaration of a global parameter for the name of the text file is the same as before.

In the OpenNLP plain text annotation format, sentences are separated by newlines. A global variable for newlines is declared as before. The template for sentences (`<xsl:template`

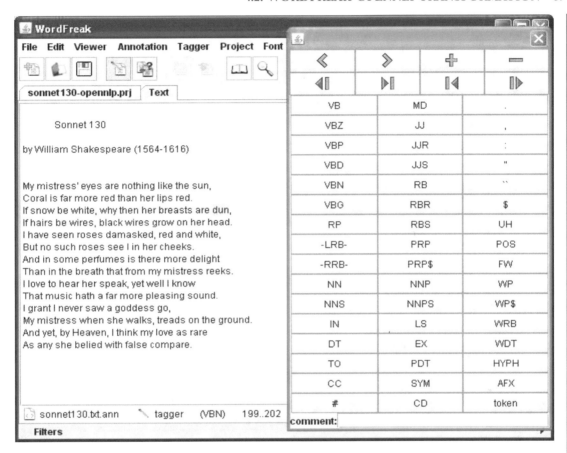

Figure 4.4: WordFreak showing *dun* tagged VBN by OpenNLP tagger.

match="Annotation[@type='sentence']"> in Figure 4.7) outputs a newline by <xsl:value-of select="$newline"/>.

In the OpenNLP plain text annotation format, words and their POS tags are separated by a slash (/). The words are obtained from the text file using XPath substring functions with the start and end values from the span attribute exactly as before, and the POS tags are obtained from the type attribute. The slash is inserted between the word and its tag by <xsl:text>/</xsl:text>, and a space is inserted before the next word/tag pair by <xsl:text> </xsl:text> as shown in Figure 4.7.

PRACTICAL WORK: TRANSFORMING WORDFREAK TO OPENNLP FORMAT

1. Analyze sonnet130.txt in WordFreak using the OpenNLP sentence detector, OpenNLP tokenizer, and OpenNLP POS tagger. Use WordFreak to manually edit the incorrect POS tags for *dun, there, reeks* and *treads*. Save the annotations file as sonnet130.txt.ann.

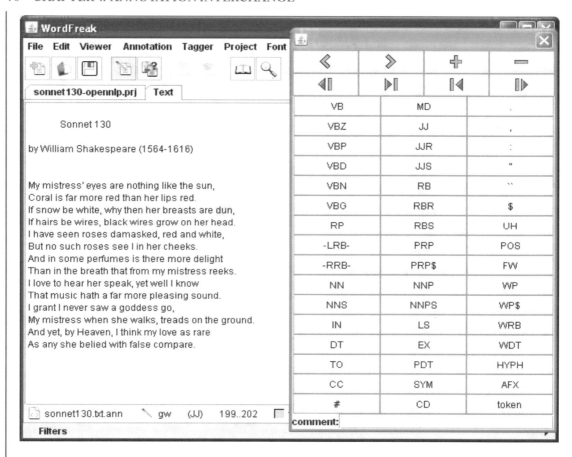

Figure 4.5: WordFreak showing *dun* tagged JJ by human editor.

2. Transform the annotations into OpenNLP plain text format using the stylesheet `wf2open.xsl` shown in Figures 4.6 and 4.7, together with the text file `sonnet130.text.xml` shown in Figure 4.1.

3. The WordFreak annotations file is the input file, and the sonnet text file is a parameter. If you use the xalan.sh script, this is done as follows:
```
./xalan.sh -in sonnet130.txt.ann -xsl wf2open.xsl
-out sonnet130.wf2open.txt -param textfile sonnet130.text.xml
```

4. The annotations should be something like Figure 4.8. Compare this with the original OpenNLP tagger annotations in Chapter 3 (Figure 3.4).

```
<xsl:stylesheet version="1.0"
  xmlns:xsl="http://www.w3.org/1999/XSL/Transform">
  <xsl:output method="text"/>
  <!-- Global parameter for text file name -->
  <xsl:param name="textfile"/>

  <!-- Global variable for newline -->
  <xsl:variable name="newline">
    <xsl:text>
</xsl:text>
  </xsl:variable>

  <xsl:template match="/">
    <xsl:apply-templates select="AnnotationFile"/>
  </xsl:template>

  <xsl:template match="AnnotationFile">
    <xsl:apply-templates />
  </xsl:template>

  <xsl:template match="Annotation[@type='file']">
    <xsl:apply-templates />
  </xsl:template>
```

Figure 4.6: `wf2open.xsl`: Transforming WordFreak to OpenNLP format (1).

4.3   GATE XML FORMAT

GATE can output annotation results in more than one format. The alternatives are described in the GATE documentation. Here we consider only the GATE XML output format.

In Chapter 1 we used GATE with `sonnet130.xml` to demonstrate the idea of stand-off annotations by adding a new layer of annotations from ANNIE to the existing layer of XML markup. Now we will use GATE with `sonnet130.txt`, the plain text version of the sonnet that we used with WordFreak in Chapter 2 and with OpenNLP in Chapter 3. This will make it easier to compare annotation formats produced by different tools for the same text. The plain text version, `sonnet130.txt`, was shown in Chapter 2 (Figure 2.3).

PRACTICAL WORK: SAVE GATE ANNOTATIONS IN XML FORMAT

1. Load `sonnet130.txt` into GATE. In detail: Select File → New language resource → GATE document. In the pop-up window, enter *sonnet130.txt* as Name, and click the browse icon to browse to `sonnet130.txt`.

```xsl
<xsl:template match="Annotation[@type='sentence']">
  <xsl:apply-templates />
  <!-- Sentences are separated by newline -->
  <xsl:value-of select="$newline"/>
</xsl:template>

<xsl:template match="Annotation">
  <!-- Get start (x) and end (y) from span="x..y" attribute -->
  <xsl:variable name="x" select="substring-before(@span,'..')"/>
  <xsl:variable name="y" select="substring-after(@span,'..')"/>
  <!-- Output word starting at x+1, of length y-x -->
  <xsl:value-of select="substring(document($textfile),
                                  $x+1, $y - $x)"/>
  <!-- Insert a / between word/tag -->
  <xsl:text>/</xsl:text>
  <!-- Output POS tag from type attribute -->
  <xsl:value-of select="@type"/>
  <!-- Output a space before next word/tag -->
  <xsl:text> </xsl:text>
</xsl:template>

<!-- Ignore anything else -->
<xsl:template match="*|@*|text()"/>
</xsl:stylesheet>
```

Figure 4.7: `wf2open.xsl`: Transforming WordFreak to OpenNLP format (2).

2. Create a GATE corpus. In detail: Select File → New language resource → GATE corpus. In the pop-up window, enter *Sonnet* as Name. Click the document list icon. Select *sonnet130.txt*, click Add and OK.

3. Load ANNIE "with defaults". In detail: Click on the ANNIE menu (the "A" icon at the top) and select With defaults.

4. Run ANNIE on the corpus. In detail: Double-click ANNIE under Applications to open an AN-NIE tab. Select the ANNIE tab and click Run.

5. View the annotations. In detail: Double-click *sonnet130.txt* under Language Resources to open a *sonnet130.txt* tab. Click Text to see the text. Click Annotation Sets to see the annotations.

6. Save the annotations in XML format. In detail: Right-click *sonnet130.txt* under Language Resources and select Save As Xml.... Output the annotations to a file named `sonnet130.gate.xml`. The contents of this file should be similar to Figures 4.9 to 4.11.

```
Sonnet/NNP 130/CD by/IN William/NNP Shakespeare/NNP (/-LRB-
 1564-1616/CD )/-RRB-
My/PRP$ mistress/NN '/POS eyes/NNS are/VBP nothing/NN like/IN
 the/DT sun/NN ,/, Coral/NNP is/VBZ far/RB more/RBR red/JJ
 than/IN her/PRP$ lips/NNS red/JJ ./.
If/IN snow/NN be/VB white/JJ ,/, why/WRB then/RB her/PRP$
 breasts/NNS are/VBP dun/JJ ,/, If/IN hairs/NNS be/VB wires/NNS
 ,/, black/JJ wires/NNS grow/VB on/IN her/PRP$ head/NN ./.
I/PRP have/VBP seen/VBN roses/NNS damasked/VBD ,/, red/JJ and/CC
 white/JJ ,/, But/CC no/DT such/JJ roses/NNS see/VBP I/PRP in/RB
 her/PRP$ cheeks/NNS ./.
And/CC in/IN some/DT perfumes/NNS is/VBZ there/EX more/JJR
 delight/NN Than/IN in/IN the/DT breath/NN that/IN from/IN
 my/PRP$ mistress/NN reeks/VBZ ./.
I/PRP love/VBP to/TO hear/VB her/PRP speak/VB ,/, yet/RB well/RB
 I/PRP know/VBP That/DT music/NN hath/VBZ a/DT far/RB more/RBR
 pleasing/JJ sound/NN ./.
I/PRP grant/VBP I/PRP never/RB saw/VBD a/DT goddess/NN go/VB ,/,
 My/PRP$ mistress/NN when/WRB she/PRP walks/VBZ ,/, treads/VBZ
 on/IN the/DT ground/NN ./.
And/CC yet/RB ,/, by/IN Heaven/NNP ,/, I/PRP think/VBP my/PRP$
 love/NN as/IN rare/JJ As/IN any/DT she/PRP belied/VBN with/IN
 false/JJ compare/NN ./.
```

Figure 4.8: `sonnet130.wf2open.txt`: OpenNLP tags corrected in WordFreak.

GATE XML FORMAT

The root element of a file in GATE XML format is `<GateDocument>`. This contains a `<GateDocumentFeatures>` element, a `<TextWithNodes>` element, and one or more `<AnnotationSet>` elements.

The `<GateDocumentFeatures>` element, shown in Figure 4.9, gives information about the annotated document. The information is represented by means of `<Feature>` elements each containing a feature `<Name>` and a feature `<Value>`. For example, the feature with name `MimeType` has value `text/plain`.

The `<TextWithNodes>` element contains the text of the annotated document. The start and end point of every token in the text is marked by a `<Node>` element, whose `id` attribute is the node's index point, as shown in Figure 4.10.

The `<AnnotationSet>` elements contain the detailed annotations. There is one `<AnnotationSet>` (the default annotation set) containing annotations added by ANNIE and another `<AnnotationSet>` for the original markups.

```
<?xml version='1.0' encoding='windows-1252'?>
<GateDocument>

<!-- The document's features-->
<GateDocumentFeatures>
<Feature>
  <Name className="java.lang.String">MimeType</Name>
  <Value className="java.lang.String">text/plain</Value>
</Feature>
<Feature>
  <Name className="java.lang.String">gate.SourceURL</Name>
  <Value className="java.lang.String">
    file:/C:/Annotations/sonnet130.txt
  </Value>
</Feature>
<Feature>
  <Name className="java.lang.String">docNewLineType</Name>
  <Value className="java.lang.String">CRLF</Value>
</Feature>
</GateDocumentFeatures>
```

Figure 4.9: `sonnet130.gate.xml`: GATE XML format (1).

Each annotation is represented by an `<Annotation>` element. An example `<Annotation>` element from the default annotation set is shown in Figure 4.11. This annotation is for a token (`Type="Token"`) starting at position 199 in the text (`StartNode="199"`) and ending at position 202 (`EndNode="199"`).

Each `<Annotation>` element contains a set of `<Feature>` elements each containing a feature `<Name>` and a feature `<Value>`. The example in Figure 4.11 shows that this token has a length feature with value 3, a string feature with value *dun*, and a category (POS tag) feature with value NN (noun).

VIEWING THE ANNOTATIONS IN GATE

The annotations can be viewed directly in the GATE graphical user interface by clicking the Annotations button. The example annotation for the token *dun* with category NN, shown in GATE XML format in Figure 4.11, is shown in the graphical interface in Figure 4.12. In this case only annotations for tokens are shown in the Annotations list, because Token is the only type selected from the Annotation Sets listed on the right.

In this example, the part-of-speech tag is incorrect. The word *dun* can be a noun, but here it is an adjective meaning brown or dusky, as we noted in Section 4.2. The correct category is JJ (adjective). One way to edit the tags is to transform GATE XML format to WordFreak XML format and then use

```
<!-- The document content area with serialized nodes -->
<TextWithNodes>
<Node id="0" />
<Node id="2" /> <Node id="3" /> <Node id="4" /> <Node id="5" /> ...
<Node id="15" />Sonnet<Node id="21" /> <Node id="22" />130 ...
<Node id="27" />
<Node id="29" />by<Node id="31" /> <Node id="32" />William ...
<Node id="65" />
<Node id="67" />
<Node id="69" />My<Node id="71" /> <Node id="72" />mistress ...
<Node id="114" />Coral<Node id="119" /> <Node id="120" />is ...
<Node id="156" />If<Node id="158" /> <Node id="159" />snow ...
<Node id="205" />If<Node id="207" /> <Node id="208" />hairs ...
<Node id="255" />I<Node id="256" /> <Node id="257" />have ...
<Node id="299" />But<Node id="302" /> <Node id="303" />no ...
<Node id="339" />And<Node id="342" /> <Node id="343" />in ...
<Node id="383" />Than<Node id="387" /> <Node id="388" />in ...
<Node id="432" />I<Node id="433" /> <Node id="434" />love ...
<Node id="475" />That<Node id="479" /> <Node id="480" />music ...
<Node id="519" />I<Node id="520" /> <Node id="521" />grant ...
<Node id="554" />My<Node id="556" /> <Node id="557" />mistress ...
<Node id="605" />And<Node id="608" /> <Node id="609" />yet ...
<Node id="650" />As<Node id="652" /> <Node id="653" />any ...
<Node id="689" />
<Node id="691" />
</TextWithNodes>
```

Figure 4.10: `sonnet130.gate.xml`: GATE XML format (2).

WordFreak to manually select the correct POS tags from the WordFreak menus. In Section 4.4, we show how to do this.

4.4   GATE-WORDFREAK TRANSFORMATION

We now describe an XSLT stylesheet that transforms GATE XML format into WordFreak XML format. The details of the stylesheet `gate2wf.xsl` are shown in Figures 4.13 to 4.15.

The stylesheet gets the words of the annotated text from the GATE XML file. A separate text file is not needed, and a parameter for the name of the text file is not needed.

The stylesheet reads annotations in GATE XML format, and writes output annotations in Word-Freak XML format. The stylesheet specifies that the output file will be in XML format by `<xsl:output method="xml"/>` in Figure 4.13.

```
<!-- The default annotation set -->
<AnnotationSet>
...
<Annotation Id="100" Type="Token" StartNode="199" EndNode="202">
<Feature>
  <Name className="java.lang.String">length</Name>
  <Value className="java.lang.String">3</Value>
</Feature>
<Feature>
  <Name className="java.lang.String">category</Name>
  <Value className="java.lang.String">NN</Value>
</Feature>
<Feature>
  <Name className="java.lang.String">orth</Name>
  <Value className="java.lang.String">lowercase</Value>
</Feature>
<Feature>
  <Name className="java.lang.String">kind</Name>
  <Value className="java.lang.String">word</Value>
</Feature>
<Feature>
  <Name className="java.lang.String">string</Name>
  <Value className="java.lang.String">dun</Value>
</Feature>
</Annotation>
...
</AnnotationSet>
```

Figure 4.11: `sonnet130.gate.xml`: `<Annotation>` showing *dun* with NN tag.

The words and their POS tags are obtained from the token annotations in the input GATE XML file. The words are obtained from the `string` attribute, and the POS tags are obtained from the `category` attribute.

The main difficulty is outputting the sentences and the tokens in the right order. This is solved in the stylesheet by looping through the sentences using `<xsl:for-each select="Annotation[@Type='Sentence']">` and sorting the sentences by their start nodes using `<xsl:sort select="@StartNode"/>`, as shown in Figure 4.14. It is important to specify `data-type="number"`, otherwise the nodes are sorted as strings (so that "10" comes before "9").

A similar `<xsl:for-each>` loop is used to process the tokens in the right order, also sorting them on their start nodes. In the case of the tokens, it is also necessary to select only those tokens that occur in

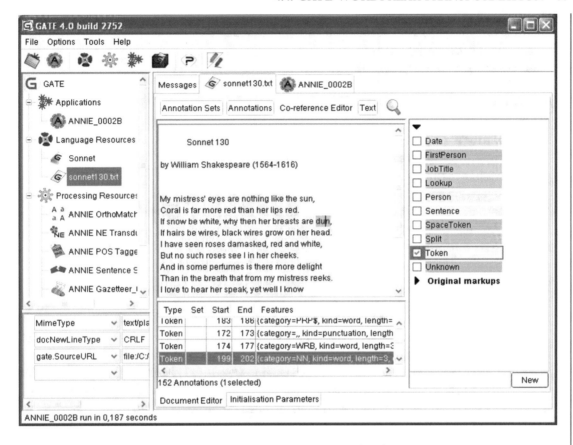

Figure 4.12: GATE and ANNIE showing *dun* tagged as Noun (NN).

each sentence, when that sentence is processed. This is done by checking that the start and end nodes of the tokens are greater than or equal to the start node of the sentence, and less than or equal to the end node of the sentence, as shown in Figure 4.14. Local variables are used for the start and end nodes of the sentences.

WordFreak XML format specifies the annotator responsible for each annotation. Normally "tagger" is used in WordFreak for automatic annotation tools, but this stylesheet sets the attribute to "GATE" as shown in Figure 4.15.

PRACTICAL WORK: TRANSFORMING GATE XML TO WORDFREAK XML

1. In Section 4.3 you analyzed sonnet130.txt with GATE and ANNIE, and saved the annotations in XML format as sonnet130.gate.xml.

2. Transform GATE XML format into WordFreak XML format using the stylesheet gate2wf.xsl shown in Figures 4.13 to 4.15.

```
<xsl:stylesheet version="1.0"
  xmlns:xsl="http://www.w3.org/1999/XSL/Transform">
  <xsl:output method="xml"/>
  <xsl:variable name="newline">
    <xsl:text>
</xsl:text>
  </xsl:variable>
  <xsl:template match="/">
    <xsl:apply-templates select="GateDocument"/>
  </xsl:template>

  <!-- Template to process top-level document element -->
  <xsl:template match="GateDocument">
    <xsl:element name="AnnotationFile">
      <xsl:attribute name="version">2.4</xsl:attribute>
      <xsl:value-of select="$newline"/>

      <xsl:element name="Annotation">
        <xsl:attribute name="type">file</xsl:attribute>
        <xsl:attribute name="span">
          <xsl:value-of select="TextWithNodes/Node[1]/@id"/>
          <xsl:text>..</xsl:text>
          <xsl:value-of select="TextWithNodes/Node[last()]/@id"/>
        </xsl:attribute>
        <xsl:attribute name="confidence">0.0</xsl:attribute>
        <xsl:attribute name="filename">
          <xsl:value-of
  select="GateDocumentFeatures/Feature[Name='gate.SourceURL']/Value"/>
          <xsl:text>.ann</xsl:text>
        </xsl:attribute>
        <xsl:attribute name="annotator">GATE</xsl:attribute>
        <xsl:attribute name="id">1</xsl:attribute>
        <xsl:value-of select="$newline"/>
        <xsl:apply-templates select="AnnotationSet"/>
      </xsl:element>
      <xsl:value-of select="$newline"/>
    </xsl:element>
  </xsl:template>
```

Figure 4.13: `gate2wf.xsl`: Transforming GATE XML to WordFreak (1).

```
<xsl:template match="AnnotationSet">
  <!-- Loop through sentences in order of StartNode -->
  <xsl:for-each select="Annotation[@Type='Sentence']">
    <xsl:sort select="@StartNode" data-type="number"/>
    <xsl:apply-templates select="."/>
  </xsl:for-each>
</xsl:template>

<!-- Template to process sentences -->
<xsl:template match="Annotation[@Type='Sentence']">
  <xsl:variable name="start" select="@StartNode"/>
  <xsl:variable name="end" select="@EndNode"/>
  <xsl:element name="Annotation">
    <xsl:attribute name="type">sentence</xsl:attribute>
    <xsl:attribute name="span">
      <xsl:value-of select="@StartNode"/>
      <xsl:text>..</xsl:text>
      <xsl:value-of select="@EndNode"/>
    </xsl:attribute>
    <xsl:attribute name="confidence">0.0</xsl:attribute>
    <xsl:attribute name="annotator">GATE</xsl:attribute>
    <xsl:attribute name="id">
      <xsl:value-of select="@Id"/>
    </xsl:attribute>
    <xsl:value-of select="$newline"/>
    <!-- Loop through tokens within sentence in order -->
    <xsl:for-each select="//Annotation[@Type='Token' and
            @StartNode>=$start and @EndNode&lt;=$end]">
      <xsl:sort select="@StartNode" data-type="number"/>
      <xsl:apply-templates select="."/>
    </xsl:for-each>
  </xsl:element>
  <xsl:value-of select="$newline"/>
</xsl:template>
```

Figure 4.14: gate2wf.xsl: Transforming GATE XML to WordFreak (2).

```
<!-- Template to process tokens -->
<xsl:template match="Annotation[@Type='Token']">
  <xsl:element name="Annotation">
    <xsl:attribute name="type">
      <xsl:value-of select="Feature[Name='category']/Value"/>
    </xsl:attribute>
    <xsl:attribute name="span">
      <xsl:value-of select="@StartNode"/>
      <xsl:text>..</xsl:text>
      <xsl:value-of select="@EndNode"/>
    </xsl:attribute>
    <xsl:attribute name="confidence">0.0</xsl:attribute>
    <xsl:attribute name="annotator">GATE</xsl:attribute>
    <xsl:attribute name="id">
      <xsl:value-of select="@Id"/>
    </xsl:attribute>
  </xsl:element>
  <xsl:value-of select="$newline"/>
</xsl:template>
</xsl:stylesheet>
```

Figure 4.15: `gate2wf.xsl`: Transforming GATE XML to WordFreak (3).

3. If you use the xalan.sh script, this is done as follows:
   ```
   ./xalan.sh -in sonnet130.gate.xml -xsl gate2wf.xsl
   -out sonnet130.txt.ann.
   ```

PRACTICAL WORK: EDITING GATE ANNOTATIONS IN WORDFREAK

1. Load `sonnet130.txt` into WordFreak with this version of `sonnet130.txt.ann` as the annotations file. To do this, put them in the same directory.

2. Click *dun* in the Text viewer. This should be similar to Figure 4.16. Note that the annotator is shown as "GATE", and the tag is NN.

3. Edit the tag for *dun* by clicking JJ in the tag menu. This should look like Figure 4.17. Note that the annotator is now "gw", and the tag is JJ.

4. Compare the GATE tags with the OpenNLP tags discussed in Section 4.2. GATE correctly tags *there* as EX, and correctly tags *treads* as VBZ, but incorrectly tags *reeks* as NNS like OpenNLP.

5. Use the WordFreak menu to edit the tags, at least for *reeks*. Save the annotations file.

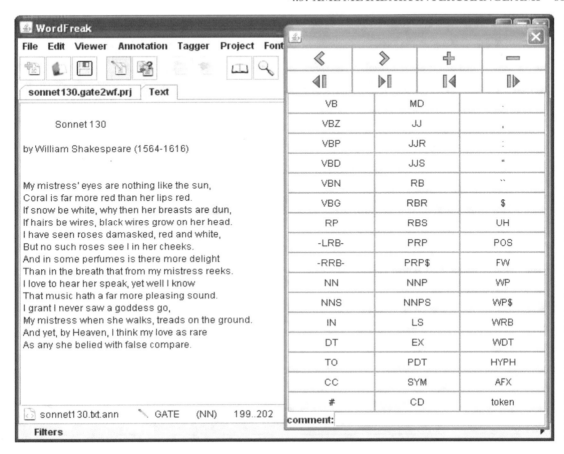

Figure 4.16: WordFreak showing *dun* tagged as Noun (NN) by GATE.

4.5   XML METADATA INTERCHANGE: XMI

As different tools produce annotations in different formats, a standard XML interchange format has been proposed in order to support the interchange of annotations. This is the XML Metadata Interchange standard (XMI). XMI is based on the Unified Modeling Language (UML), and provides an XML exchange format for UML models. In order to support XMI as a standard, its specifications are the responsibility of the OMG (Object Management Group) organization. The formal specification for XMI is available from OMG at `http://www.omg.org/technology/documents/formal/xmi.htm`.

OPENNLP ANNOTATIONS IN XMI FORMAT

XMI format is used by the UIMA architecture described in Chapter 5. Some annotations of `sonnet130.txt` in XMI format are shown in Figures 4.18 to 4.20. These were produced by running OpenNLP tools in UIMA.

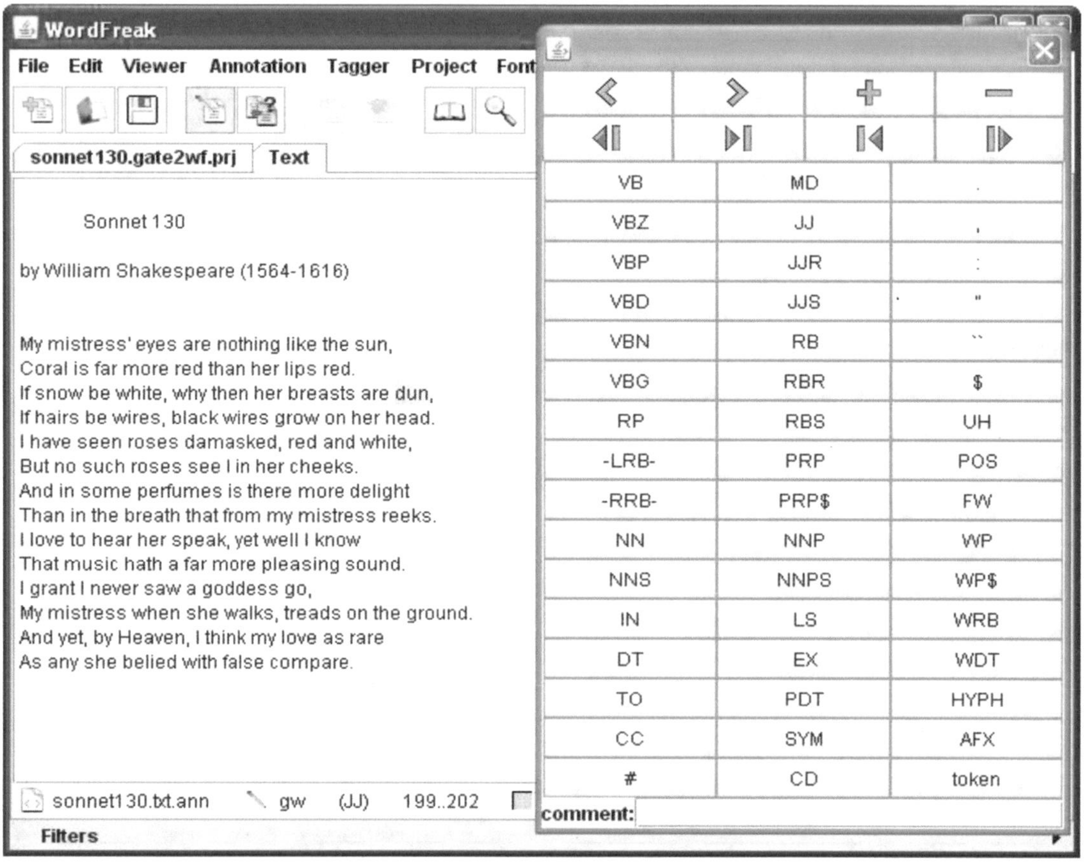

Figure 4.17: WordFreak showing *dun* tagged JJ by human editor.

In UIMA, the overall annotation structure is called the *Common Analysis Structure* (CAS). The UIMA CAS namespace is declared in the root element <xmi:XMI> by the attribute xmlns:cas="http:///uima/cas.ecore". The text is included in the CAS as well as the stand-off annotations that refer to it. In UIMA, the text to be annotated is called the *Subject of Analysis* (SofA). Figure 4.18 shows the text of Sonnet 130 as the string value of the sofaString attribute of the <cas:Sofa> element.

The annotations by OpenNLP Sentence Detector are shown in Figure 4.19. The <opennlp:Sentence> elements have the opennlp namespace prefix, as they belong to the UIMA examples OpenNLP namespace declared in Figure 4.18. In principle there could be other Sentence annotations from some other namespace. The sentence boundaries are marked by specifying their begin and end points. These indices are relative to a specified Subject of Analysis, in this case sofa="1". The source of the annotation is given (rather verbosely) by componentId="OpenNLP Sentence Detector".

```
<?xml version="1.0" encoding="UTF-8"?>
<xmi:XMI
  xmlns:opennlp="http:///org/apache/uima/examples/opennlp.ecore"
  xmlns:tcas="http:///uima/tcas.ecore"
  xmlns:cas="http:///uima/cas.ecore"
  xmlns:examples="http:///org/apache/uima/examples.ecore"
  xmlns:xmi="http://www.omg.org/XMI" xmi:version="2.0">
<cas:NULL xmi:id="0"/>
<cas:Sofa xmi:id="1" sofaNum="1" sofaID="_InitialView"
  mimetype="text" sofaString="
              Sonnet 130

by William Shakespeare (1564-1616)


My mistress' eyes are nothing like the sun,
Coral is far more red than her lips red.
If snow be white, why then her breasts are dun,
If hairs be wires, black wires grow on her head.
I have seen roses damasked, red and white,
But no such roses see I in her cheeks.
And in some perfumes is there more delight
Than in the breath that from my mistress reeks.
I love to hear her speak, yet well I know
That music hath a far more pleasing sound.
I grant I never saw a goddess go,
My mistress when she walks, treads on the ground.
And yet, by Heaven, I think my love as rare
As any she belied with false compare.
"/>
```

Figure 4.18: sonnet130.txt.xmi: XML Metadata Interchange format (1).

```
<tcas:DocumentAnnotation xmi:id="999998"
  sofa="1" begin="0" end="673" language="en"/>
<examples:SourceDocumentInformation xmi:id="999999"
  sofa="1" begin="0" end="0"
  uri="file:/C:\Annotations\sonnet130.txt" offsetInSource="0"
  documentSize="673" lastSegment="true"/>
<opennlp:Sentence xmi:id="2" sofa="1" begin="0" end="147"
  componentId="OpenNLP Sentence Detector"/>
<opennlp:Sentence xmi:id="31" sofa="1" begin="148" end="245"
  componentId="OpenNLP Sentence Detector"/>
<opennlp:Sentence xmi:id="56" sofa="1" begin="246" end="327"
  componentId="OpenNLP Sentence Detector"/>
<opennlp:Sentence xmi:id="77" sofa="1" begin="328" end="419"
  componentId="OpenNLP Sentence Detector"/>
<opennlp:Sentence xmi:id="96" sofa="1" begin="420" end="504"
  componentId="OpenNLP Sentence Detector"/>
<opennlp:Sentence xmi:id="117" sofa="1" begin="505" end="589"
  componentId="OpenNLP Sentence Detector"/>
<opennlp:Sentence xmi:id="138" sofa="1" begin="590" end="672"
  componentId="OpenNLP Sentence Detector"/>
...
```

Figure 4.19: `sonnet130.txt.xmi`: XML Metadata Interchange format (2).

The OpenNLP Tokenizer has marked the token boundaries in the same way in the `<opennlp:Token>` elements in Figure 4.20. The OpenNLP POS Tagger has added `posTag` attributes to the tokens. The examples in Figure 4.20 show the POS tags for *My mistress' eyes are nothing like the sun*. The source of the annotations remains `componentId="OpenNLP Tokenizer"`, despite the addition of the `posTag` attributes by the OpenNLP POS Tagger.

Although XMI has not yet been widely adopted as a standard, it will be important because it is the format used by UIMA. We therefore give an example of how to do transformations from other formats to XMI: Section 4.6 shows how to transform WordFreak annotations to XMI format.

4.6 WORDFREAK-XMI TRANSFORMATION

The stylesheet shown in Figures 4.21 to 4.25 transforms WordFreak XML format to UIMA XMI format. This example works for annotations at the sentence, token and POS tag levels, but not for higher levels.

Unlike the stylesheets discussed earlier, `wf2uima.xsl` has a large number of namespace declarations at the beginning (Figure 4.21). These include the XMI namespace, and also namespaces for the UIMA CAS (Common Analysis Structure) and for the OpenNLP annotations.

```
...
<opennlp:Token xmi:id="11" sofa="1" begin="63" end="65"
  posTag="PRP$" componentId="OpenNLP Tokenizer"/>
<opennlp:Token xmi:id="12" sofa="1" begin="66" end="74"
  posTag="NN" componentId="OpenNLP Tokenizer"/>
<opennlp:Token xmi:id="13" sofa="1" begin="74" end="75"
  posTag="POS" componentId="OpenNLP Tokenizer"/>
<opennlp:Token xmi:id="14" sofa="1" begin="76" end="80"
  posTag="NNS" componentId="OpenNLP Tokenizer"/>
<opennlp:Token xmi:id="15" sofa="1" begin="81" end="84"
  posTag="VBP" componentId="OpenNLP Tokenizer"/>
<opennlp:Token xmi:id="16" sofa="1" begin="85" end="92"
  posTag="NN" componentId="OpenNLP Tokenizer"/>
<opennlp:Token xmi:id="17" sofa="1" begin="93" end="97"
  posTag="IN" componentId="OpenNLP Tokenizer"/>
<opennlp:Token xmi:id="18" sofa="1" begin="98" end="101"
  posTag="DT" componentId="OpenNLP Tokenizer"/>
<opennlp:Token xmi:id="19" sofa="1" begin="102" end="105"
  posTag="NN" componentId="OpenNLP Tokenizer"/>
<opennlp:Token xmi:id="20" sofa="1" begin="105" end="106"
  posTag="," componentId="OpenNLP Tokenizer"/>
...
<cas:View sofa="1" members="999998 999999 2 3 4 5...
  ...155 156 157 158"/>
</xmi:XMI>
```

Figure 4.20: `sonnet130.txt.xmi`: XML Metadata Interchange format (3).

As WordFreak XML format does not include the text, a global parameter is used to obtain the name of an XML file containing the text. A global variable containing a newline is declared so that newlines can be inserted into the output to improve readability. These methods were described in Section 4.1.

The template in Figure 4.22 builds the overall structure of the output XMI file, by creating the root element `<xmi:XMI>`, by creating the `<cas:Sofa>` and `<cas:View>` elements inside `<xmi:XMI>`, and by using `<apply-templates />` to produce the detailed annotations in between. The `<cas:Sofa>` element includes the `<sofaString>` attribute, whose value is the complete text, obtained from the text file by `<xsl:value-of select="document($textfile)"/>`.

The `<cas:View>` element includes a `members` attribute, whose value is a list of `xmi:id` numbers. Only annotations whose `xmi:id` numbers are listed as members of the view will be shown when the view is displayed, for example by the UIMA Annotation Viewer. The template in Figure 4.22 collects the list of `xmi:id` numbers for all annotation types (except `file`) by means of an `<xsl:for-each>` loop.

```
<xsl:stylesheet version="1.0"
  xmlns:xsl="http://www.w3.org/1999/XSL/Transform"
  xmlns:examples="http:///org/apache/uima/examples.ecore"
  xmlns:cas="http:///uima/cas.ecore"
  xmlns:tcas="http:///uima/tcas.ecore"
  xmlns:opennlp="http:///org/apache/uima/examples/opennlp.ecore"
  xmlns:xmi="http://www.omg.org/XMI">
  <xsl:output method="xml"/>
  <!-- Global parameter for text file name -->
  <xsl:param name="textfile"/>

  <!-- Global variable for newline -->
  <xsl:variable name="newline">
    <xsl:text>
</xsl:text>
  </xsl:variable>

  <xsl:template match="/">
    <xsl:apply-templates select="AnnotationFile"/>
  </xsl:template>
```

Figure 4.21: `wf2uima.xsl`: Transforming WordFreak to UIMA XMI (1).

The `<apply-templates />` in Figure 4.22 causes the template in Figure 4.23 to be executed. This template inserts a `<tcas:DocumentAnnotation>` element and `<examples:SourceDocumentInformation>` element after the `<cas:Sofa>` element. It then inserts all the sentence annotations by `<apply-templates>`, followed by the token annotations by means of another `<apply-templates>`. These annotations come before the `<cas:View>` element created in Figure 4.22.

The sentence annotations are handled by the template in Figure 4.24. An `<opennlp:Sentence>` element is created for each WordFreak sentence annotation. The values of the begin and end attributes are extracted from the WordFreak span attribute using XPath substring functions. The value of the componentId attribute is copied from the WordFreak annotator attribute, unless it is "tagger" in which case it is replaced by the more informative "OpenNLP Sentence Detector".

The token annotations are handled by the template in Figure 4.25, which is very similar to the sentence template in Figure 4.24. An `<opennlp:Token>` element is created for each WordFreak token annotation. The values of the begin and end attributes are extracted from the WordFreak span attribute using XPath substring functions. The value of the posTag attribute is copied from the WordFreak type attribute. Note that if the token has not been tagged, the value of the WordFreak type attribute is "token" and this is also copied to posTag. The value of the componentId attribute is copied from the WordFreak annotator attribute, unless it is "tagger" in which case it is replaced by the more informative "OpenNLP Tokenizer".

```
<!-- Template to process top-level document element -->
<xsl:template match="AnnotationFile">
  <xsl:element name="xmi:XMI">
    <xsl:attribute name="xmi:version">2.0</xsl:attribute>
      <xsl:value-of select="$newline"/>

      <xsl:element name="cas:NULL">
        <xsl:attribute name="xmi:id">0</xsl:attribute>
      </xsl:element>
      <xsl:value-of select="$newline"/>
      <xsl:element name="cas:Sofa">
        <xsl:attribute name="xmi:id">1</xsl:attribute>
        <xsl:attribute name="sofaNum">1</xsl:attribute>
        <xsl:attribute name="sofaID">_InitialView</xsl:attribute>
        <xsl:attribute name="mimetype">text</xsl:attribute>
        <xsl:attribute name="sofaString">
          <xsl:value-of select="document($textfile)"/>
        </xsl:attribute>
      </xsl:element>
      <xsl:value-of select="$newline"/>

      <xsl:apply-templates />
      <xsl:element name="cas:View">
        <xsl:attribute name="sofa">1</xsl:attribute>
        <xsl:attribute name="members">
          <xsl:text>999998</xsl:text>
          <xsl:text> </xsl:text>
          <xsl:text>999999</xsl:text>
          <xsl:for-each select="//Annotation[@type!='file']">
            <xsl:text> </xsl:text>
            <xsl:value-of select="@id"/>
          </xsl:for-each>
        </xsl:attribute>
      </xsl:element>
      <xsl:value-of select="$newline"/>

  </xsl:element>
</xsl:template>
```

Figure 4.22: wf2uima.xsl: Transforming WordFreak to UIMA XMI (2).

```
<!-- Template to process document information -->
<xsl:template match="Annotation[@type='file']">
  <xsl:element name="tcas:DocumentAnnotation">
    <xsl:attribute name="xmi:id">999998</xsl:attribute>
    <xsl:attribute name="sofa">1</xsl:attribute>
    <xsl:attribute name="begin">
      <xsl:value-of select="substring-before(@span,'..')"/>
    </xsl:attribute>
    <xsl:attribute name="end">
      <xsl:value-of select="substring-after(@span,'..')"/>
    </xsl:attribute>
    <xsl:attribute name="language">en</xsl:attribute>
  </xsl:element>
  <xsl:value-of select="$newline"/>

  <xsl:element name="examples:SourceDocumentInformation">
    <xsl:attribute name="xmi:id">999999</xsl:attribute>
    <xsl:attribute name="sofa">1</xsl:attribute>
    <xsl:attribute name="begin">0</xsl:attribute>
    <xsl:attribute name="end">0</xsl:attribute>
    <xsl:attribute name="uri">
      <xsl:text>file:/</xsl:text>
      <xsl:value-of select="substring-before(@filename,'.ann')"/>
    </xsl:attribute>
    <xsl:attribute name="offsetInSource">
      <xsl:value-of select="substring-before(@span,'..')"/>
    </xsl:attribute>
    <xsl:attribute name="documentSize">
      <xsl:value-of select="substring-after(@span,'..')"/>
    </xsl:attribute>
    <xsl:attribute name="lastSegment">true</xsl:attribute>
  </xsl:element>
  <xsl:value-of select="$newline"/>

  <xsl:apply-templates select="Annotation[@type='sentence']"/>
  <xsl:apply-templates select="Annotation[@type='sentence']/Annotation"/>
</xsl:template>
```

Figure 4.23: `wf2uima.xsl`: Transforming WordFreak to UIMA XMI (3).

```
<!-- Template to process sentences -->
<xsl:template match="Annotation[@type='sentence']">
  <xsl:element name="opennlp:Sentence">
    <xsl:attribute name="xmi:id">
      <xsl:value-of select="@id"/>
    </xsl:attribute>
    <xsl:attribute name="sofa">1</xsl:attribute>
    <xsl:attribute name="begin">
      <xsl:value-of select="substring-before(@span,'..')"/>
    </xsl:attribute>
    <xsl:attribute name="end">
      <xsl:value-of select="substring-after(@span,'..')"/>
    </xsl:attribute>
    <xsl:attribute name="componentId">
      <xsl:choose>
        <xsl:when test="@annotator='tagger'">
          <xsl:text>OpenNLP Sentence Detector</xsl:text>
        </xsl:when>
        <xsl:otherwise>
          <xsl:value-of select="@annotator"/>
        </xsl:otherwise>
      </xsl:choose>
    </xsl:attribute>
  </xsl:element>
  <xsl:value-of select="$newline"/>
</xsl:template>
```

Figure 4.24: wf2uima.xsl: Transforming WordFreak to UIMA XMI (4).

PRACTICAL WORK: TRANSFORMING WORDFREAK TO UIMA FORMAT

1. The stylesheet shown in Figures 4.21 to 4.25 transforms WordFreak XML format to UIMA XMI format.

2. Use it like this to transform sonnet130.txt.ann:
   ./xalan.sh -in sonnet130.txt.ann -xsl wf2uima.xsl
   -out sonnet130.wf2uima.xmi -param textfile sonnet130.text.xml.

3. The transformed annotations can be viewed with UIMA Annotation Viewer as shown in Figure 4.27.

```xsl
<!-- Template to process tokens -->
<xsl:template match="Annotation">
  <xsl:element name="opennlp:Token">
    <xsl:attribute name="xmi:id">
      <xsl:value-of select="@id"/>
    </xsl:attribute>
    <xsl:attribute name="sofa">1</xsl:attribute>
    <xsl:attribute name="begin">
      <xsl:value-of select="substring-before(@span,'..')"/>
    </xsl:attribute>
    <xsl:attribute name="end">
      <xsl:value-of select="substring-after(@span,'..')"/>
    </xsl:attribute>
    <xsl:attribute name="posTag">
      <xsl:value-of select="@type"/>
    </xsl:attribute>
    <xsl:attribute name="componentId">
      <xsl:choose>
        <xsl:when test="@annotator='tagger'">
          <xsl:text>OpenNLP Tokenizer</xsl:text>
        </xsl:when>
        <xsl:otherwise>
          <xsl:value-of select="@annotator"/>
        </xsl:otherwise>
      </xsl:choose>
    </xsl:attribute>
  </xsl:element>
  <xsl:value-of select="$newline"/>
</xsl:template>

<xsl:template match="*|@*|text()"/>
</xsl:stylesheet>
```

Figure 4.25: `wf2uima.xsl`: Transforming WordFreak to UIMA XMI (5).

VIEWING XMI ANNOTATIONS

To view annotations in XMI format we can use UIMA Annotation Viewer. For this purpose no knowledge about the UIMA architecture is required, or about how to create annotations using UIMA. The Annotation Viewer is started by the `annotationViewer.sh` script (or the equivalent `annotationViewer.bat` file) provided in the UIMA `bin` directory.

The script opens a window like Figure 4.26. For Input Directory, browse to the directory containing the annotation files. For TypeSystem or AE Descriptor File, browse to `OpenNLPExampleTypes.xml`. This is found in a subdirectory of `opennlp_wrappers/src` in the directory where UIMA examples are installed, as shown in Figure 4.26.

Click View to see a list of files in the directory, and double-click the file to be viewed. The OpenNLP sonnet annotations shown in XMI format in Figures 4.18 to 4.20 can be viewed in Chapter 5, in Figure 5.16.

Recall that *dun* is incorrectly tagged VBN by OpenNLP POS tagger. This was discussed in Section 4.2, which showed how to correct the OpenNLP tags in WordFreak and transform them to OpenNLP format. Now, we can run OpenNLP tagger in WordFreak, edit the tags in WordFreak, and transform them to XMI format with the WordFreak-XMI transformation. The result is shown in Figure 4.27. Note that the `componentId` for *dun* is "gw".

4.7 TOWARDS INTEROPERABILITY

In general, the possibility of different annotation tools working together and interchanging annotations is known as *interoperability*. Several research workshops (Webster et al. 2008, Hahn 2008) have recently been devoted to making progress towards this important goal.

In this chapter, we showed that by using XSLT transformations between different annotation formats, we can achieve a certain level of *interoperability of annotations*. However, this still leaves the user of the annotation tools with all the responsibility for managing the annotation formats within the overall annotation system. The user has to understand the details of different XML formats, and write new XSLT stylesheets if necessary. The user also has to organize the overall flow of processing between components, including not only the annotation components that actually create annotations but also the transformation components that merely transform between formats.

In order to relieve the user of these responsibilities, so the user can focus on the annotations themselves rather than their formats, we need a better approach that aims to achieve *interoperability of annotation tools*. It should be possible for the user to select appropriate annotation tools for different purposes, and to assume that the tools will pass their annotations along from one tool to the next tool without worrying about the format details. This has been the motivation for the development of *annotation architectures*, the topic of Chapter 5.

In fact, we saw a good example of interoperability of annotation tools with OpenNLP in Chapter 3. The OpenNLP tools are designed to work together, in such a way that the output of one tool is the input for the next tool. The task of organizing the overall flow of processing between several components is managed for OpenNLP by Linux shell scripts, as seen in the practical work in Chapter 3. Piping the output of one tool into the next by means of the Linux pipe (shown by the "|" symbol in the scripts) is very simple and extremely efficient. However, all these tools come from the same toolkit, so it is not surprising that they work together so successfully. An annotation architecture should provide support for combining tools that come from different backgrounds.

Although the user of the tools should not be required to know the XML format details, it is important to maintain a clear check on the *content* and *type* of the annotations at different levels. For

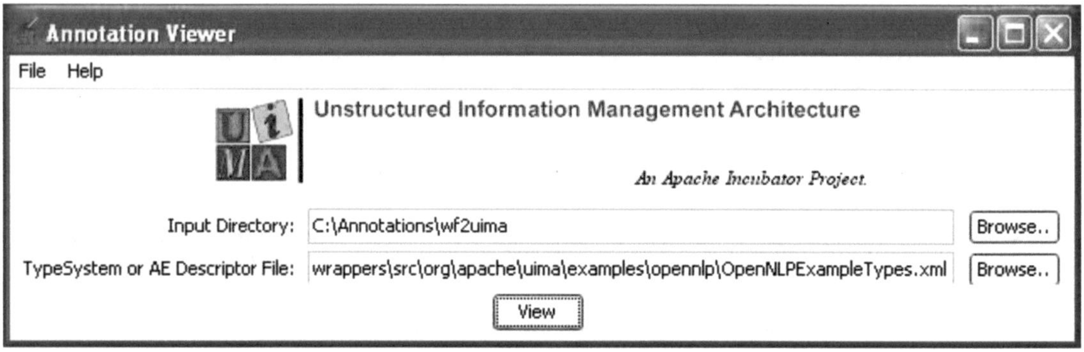

Figure 4.26: UIMA Annotation Viewer with OpenNLPExampleTypes.xml.

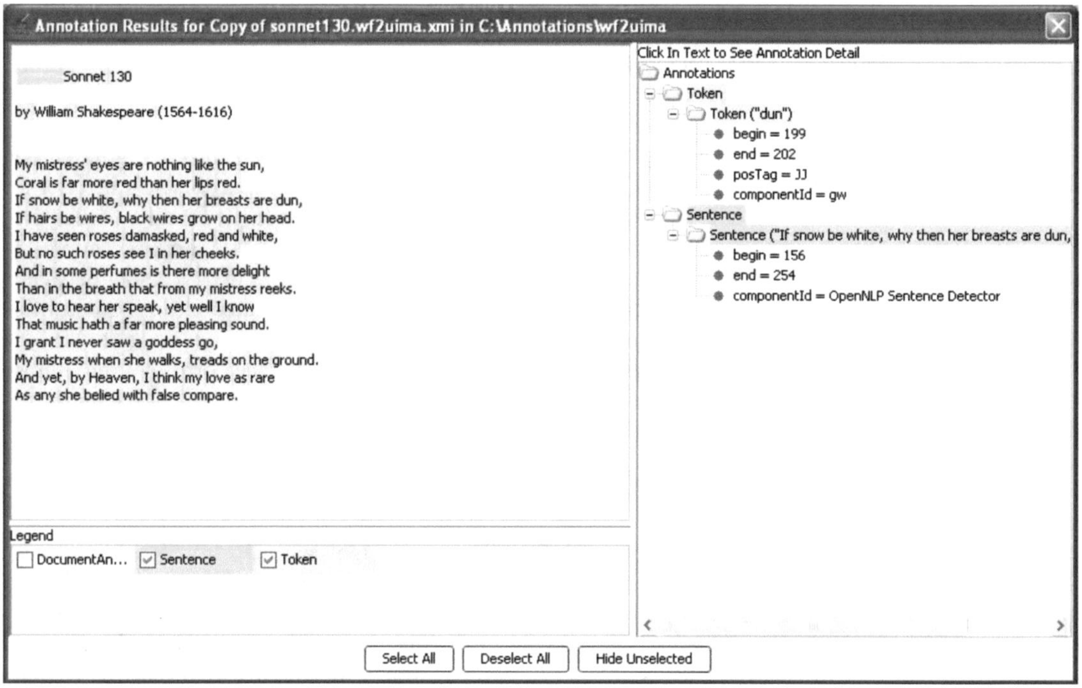

Figure 4.27: UIMA Annotation Viewer showing *dun* edited to JJ in WordFreak.

example, a tokenizer's output consists of segmented but untagged tokens, and likewise a tagger's input consists of segmented but untagged tokens. So the annotations that are output from the tokenizer are basically the right type to serve as the input to the tagger. It is possible to automatically check that the types of the annotations output from one component are the right types for input to the next component. This can be done by means of a *type system* for annotations, as we will see in Chapter 5.

4.8   FURTHER READING

- XSLT transformations: See (Tidwell 2001).

- XML Metadata Interchange standard: See
  http://www.omg.org/technology/documents/formal/xmi.htm.

- Interoperability: See (Webster et al. 2008) and (Hahn 2008).

CHAPTER 5

Annotation Architectures

As discussed in Section 4.7, the need for interoperability of annotation tools was a motivation for the development of annotation architectures. In this chapter, we describe two annotation architectures, GATE and UIMA. Note that as both GATE and UIMA have extensive documentation, the examples will not give such detailed instructions as for WordFreak and OpenNLP.

To facilitate comparison, the descriptions have the same structure. First, the architectures are introduced (GATE in Section 5.1 and UIMA in Section 5.5). Second, as the architectures include a set of ready-to-run linguistic annotation tools these are described next (ANNIE information extraction tools for GATE in Section 5.2 and UIMA wrappers for OpenNLP tools in Section 5.6). Third, facilities for rule-based annotations are presented (GATE's JAPE rules in Section 5.3 and UIMA's regular expression annotators in Section 5.7). Fourth, we show how to customize name lists for named entity lookup (GATE gazetteers in Section 5.4 and UIMA dictionaries in Section 5.8).

5.1 GATE

General Architecture for Text Engineering (GATE) was developed at University of Sheffield over many years (Cunningham et al. 2002). The maturity of the software means that GATE (http://www.gate.ac.uk) is a robust and reliable platform that has been used successfully in a large number of projects. We introduced GATE in Chapter 1 and described GATE XML format in Chapter 4. We now consider GATE as an architecture, and review the facilities that it provides in order to support the user in organizing annotation tasks.

The GATE architecture distinguishes two basic kinds of resources: *Language Resources* and *Processing Resources*. A Language Resource can be an individual text, loaded as a *GATE Document*, or a collection of texts, loaded as a *GATE Corpus*. As we saw in Chapter 1, when a text is loaded as a GATE Document, the text is separated from its markup using standoff annotations. A Processing Resource is a distinct processing component such as a tokenizer or a named entity recognizer. An *Application* is a collection of Processing Resources organized into a processing pipeline. An Application can be named and saved. A saved Application can be quickly reloaded into GATE together with its associated Processing Resources and Language Resources.

GATE provides a very wide range of components for many kinds of tasks. We show how to configure these components in Section 5.2. Annotations can also be created with user-defined pattern-matching rules, called JAPE rules. This allows rapid development of new components without the need for Java programming. We show how to define rule-based annotation components in Section 5.3. GATE also provides a wide range of name lists (gazetteers) for named entity lookup. We show how to customize gazetteers in Section 5.4.

GETTING STARTED WITH GATE AND ANNIE

It's easy to get started using GATE via its own graphical user interface (Figure 5.1), as we saw in Chapter 1. This interface can be used directly by non-programmers who want to immediately start annotating texts for themselves. In addition, Java programmers who are developing text analytics applications for end users can embed GATE components in their applications via a Java API.

Another advantage of GATE is that it includes a ready-to-run information extraction system, ANNIE. We start by repeating the practical exercise from Chapter 4. For more detailed instructions, see Section 4.3.

PRACTICAL WORK: GATE AND ANNIE

1. Load `sonnet130.txt` into GATE.

2. Create a GATE corpus *Sonnet* containing `sonnet130.txt`.

3. Load ANNIE "with defaults".

4. Run ANNIE on the corpus and view the annotations (Figure 5.1).

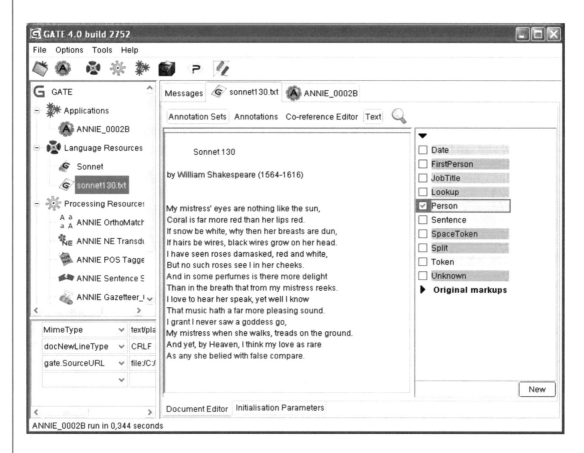

Figure 5.1: GATE named entity recognition: Person annotations.

5.2   GATE INFORMATION EXTRACTION TOOLS

CONFIGURING ANNIE COMPONENTS IN GATE

A sentence splitter, tokenizer, POS tagger, gazetteer lookup, and named entity recognizer are included when ANNIE is loaded with defaults. Other processing components such as nominal and pronominal coreference can easily be added to the ANNIE pipeline using GATE's graphical user interface.

PRACTICAL WORK: ADDING ANNIE NOMINAL COREFERENCER

1. From the New Processing Resource menu (the cogwheel icon at the top), select *ANNIE Nominal Coreferencer*.

2. In ANNIE, add the Nominal Coreferencer to the end of the pipeline by clicking the ">>" button. This step is shown in Figure 5.2.

3. Run ANNIE on the *Sonnet* corpus and view the annotations.

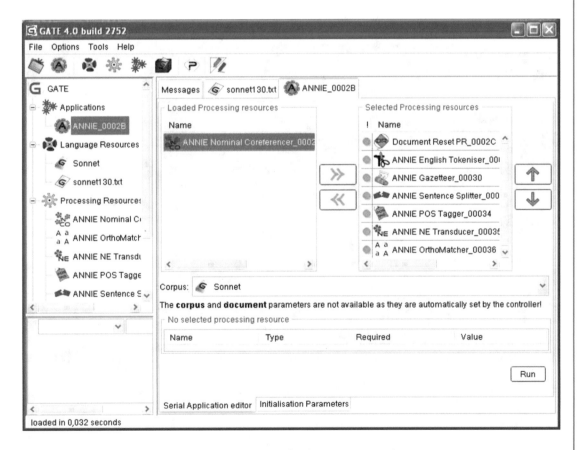

Figure 5.2: GATE: Adding the Nominal Coreference component to ANNIE.

PRACTICAL WORK: ADDING ANNIE PRONOMINAL COREFERENCER

1. From the New Processing Resource menu (the cogwheel icon at the top), select *ANNIE Pronominal Coreferencer*.

2. In ANNIE, add the Pronominal Coreferencer to the end of the pipeline.

3. Run ANNIE on the *Sonnet* corpus again.

4. View the annotations made by ANNIE including the new components. They should be similar to Figure 5.3.

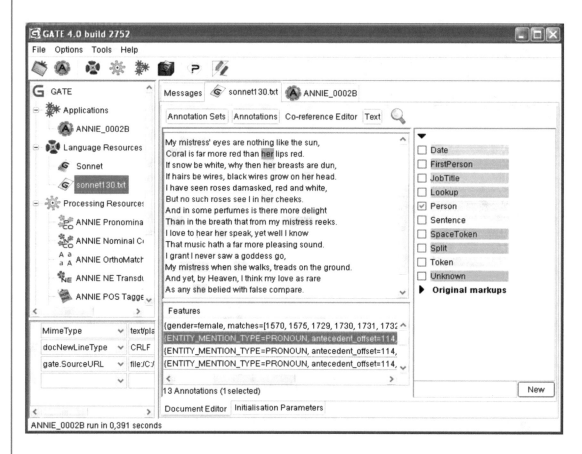

Figure 5.3: GATE coreference: ANNIE Pronominal Coreferencer.

CONFIGURING OTHER COMPONENTS IN GATE

The ANNIE nominal and pronominal coreference components are ready for loading from the New Processing Resource menu. Many other processing components are available with GATE (see Figure 5.4), but before they can be loaded they need to be added to the New Processing Resource menu. This is easily done using GATE's graphical user interface.

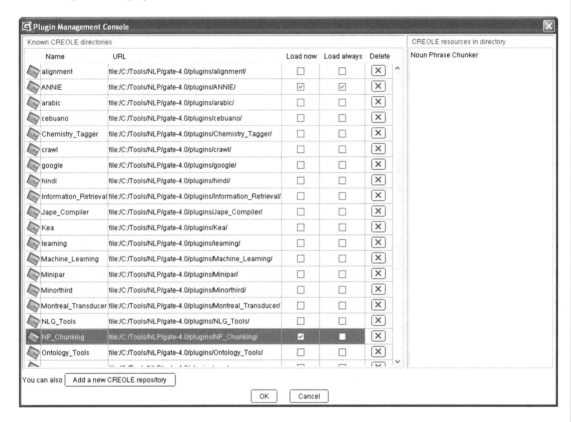

Figure 5.4: GATE: Loading the Noun Phrase Chunker component.

PRACTICAL WORK: ADDING NOUN PHRASE CHUNKER

1. From the File menu at the top, select *Manage CREOLE plugins*.

2. In the Plugin Management Console window, select *NP_Chunking* and click *Load now*. This step is shown in Figure 5.4.

3. From the main GATE window's New Processing Resource menu (the cogwheel icon at the top), select *Noun Phrase Chunker*.

4. In ANNIE, add the Noun Phrase Chunker to the end of the pipeline by clicking the ">>" button.

5. Run ANNIE on the *Sonnet* corpus and view the NounChunk annotations made by the new component. They should be similar to Figure 5.5.

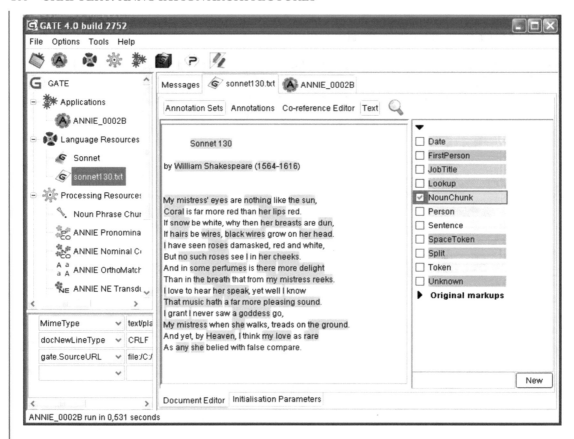

Figure 5.5: GATE chunking: Noun Phrase Chunker.

5.3   ANNOTATIONS WITH JAPE RULES

GATE provides an easy way to add customizable annotations without the need for programming. JAPE is a system for writing annotation rules that check for patterns in annotations created by other components and add new annotations if the patterns are found.

JAPE RULES FOR NP

As an example, Figure 5.6 shows some simple JAPE rules for noun phrases. The annotations made by these rules are approximately the same as those made by the GATE Noun Phrase Chunker, but the JAPE rules are user-written and therefore highly customizable.

JAPE rules are organized into phases: these rules belong to the NP phase (Phase: NP). The rules specify what kind of input they work on: these rules work on tokens (Input: Token) and have no effect on any other kind of input.

The left-hand sides of the rules specify the conditions. In these examples, the conditions are simple tag patterns checking for the presence of particular sequences of POS tags in the annotated tokens.

```
Phase: NP
Input: Token

Rule: NP1
(
  ({Token.category == "DT"}|{Token.category == "PRP$"})?
  ({Token.category == "RB"}|{Token.category == "RBR"})*
  ({Token.category == "JJ"}|{Token.category == "JJR"})*
  ({Token.category == "NN"}|{Token.category == "NNS"})+
)
:nounPhrase -->
  :nounPhrase.NP = {kind="NP", rule=NP1}

Rule: NP2
(
  ({Token.category == "NNP"})+
)
:nounPhrase -->
  :nounPhrase.NP = {kind="NP", rule=NP2}

Rule: NP3
(
  ({Token.category == "DT"})?
  ({Token.category == "PRP"})
)
:nounPhrase -->
  :nounPhrase.NP = {kind="NP", rule=NP3}
```

Figure 5.6: GATE: JAPE rules for Noun Phrases.

Rule NP2, the simplest, says that one or more proper nouns (tokens tagged NNP, with "+" for one or more) are to be annotated as a noun phrase NP.

Rule NP1 uses regular expressions to specify the tag patterns: an optional determiner DT or possessive pronoun PRP$ (with "|" for disjunction and "?" for optional), followed by zero or more adverbs RB or RBR (with "*" for zero or more), followed by zero or more adjectives JJ or JJR (with "*" for zero or more), followed non-optionally by one or more singular or plural nouns NN or NNS (with "+" for one or more). Any token sequence matching this tag pattern is to be annotated as a noun phrase NP.

Rule NP3 allows a personal pronoun PRP to be an NP. Unusually, it also allows the pronoun to be optionally preceded by a determiner DT. In Sonnet 130, this rule correctly annotates *any she* in the last line as a noun phrase.

PRACTICAL WORK: JAPE RULES FOR NP

1. Copy Figure 5.6 into a file NP.jape, or write your own JAPE rules.

2. Use the same GATE corpus *Sonnet* with sonnet130.txt in it as before.

3. Load ANNIE "with defaults". Then load NP.jape as a new processing resource and add it to the end of the ANNIE pipeline.

4. Run ANNIE on the *Sonnet* corpus.

5. View the NP annotations made by the JAPE rules. They should be similar to Figure 5.7. Compare these NPs with the chunker NPs in Figure 5.5.

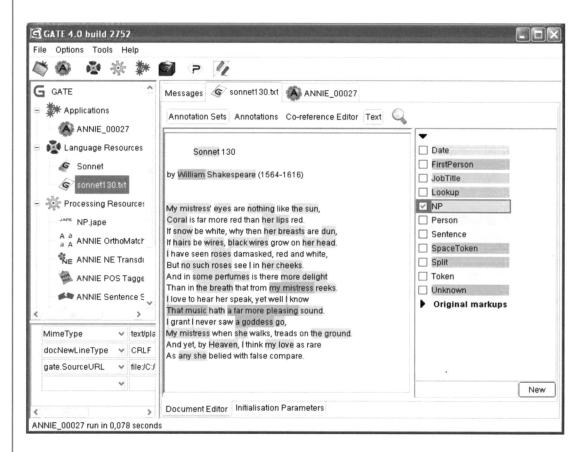

Figure 5.7: GATE: Noun Phrases annotated by JAPE rules.

```
Phase:PP
Input: Token NP

Rule: PP1
(
  {Token.category == "IN"}
  {NP.kind == "NP"}
)
:prepPhrase -->
  :prepPhrase.PP = {kind="PP", rule=PP1}
```

Figure 5.8: GATE: JAPE rule for Prepositional Phrases.

JAPE RULES FOR PP
A JAPE rule to annotate prepositional phrases is shown in Figure 5.8. This rule belongs to the PP phase (`Phase: PP`) which needs to be executed after the NP phase, because this rule works on both tokens and noun phrases (`Input: Token NP`).

Rule PP1 says that a sequence of a preposition (a token tagged as IN) followed by a noun phrase (which has already been annotated as NP) is to be annotated as a prepositional phrase PP. This is an example of cascaded chunking: the PP phase works by taking as its input the results of the NP phase.

Note that the Penn Treebank tag IN is used for subordinating conjunctions such as *if* as well as for prepositions. As a result, sequences such as *if snow* are incorrectly annotated as prepositional phrases by this rule.

PRACTICAL WORK: JAPE RULES FOR PP
1. Copy Figure 5.8 into a file `PP.jape`, or write your own JAPE rules.

2. Load `PP.jape` as a new processing resource and add it to the end of the ANNIE pipeline, after `NP.jape`.

3. Run ANNIE again on the *Sonnet* corpus.

4. View the annotations added by ANNIE. They should include new PP annotations as shown in Figure 5.9.

5.4   CUSTOMIZING GATE GAZETTEERS
GATE includes a large number of name lists, called gazetteers, that support named entity recognition. Some of the lists can be seen in the middle column in Figure 5.10. The ANNIE gazetteer component matches words in the text with items in the lists and annotates them with the relevant categories. We now show how this lookup process can be customized.

CUSTOMIZING A GAZETTEER IN GATE

The first level of customization is deciding which lists will be used during the lookup process. All the lists that are provided with GATE are in the directory `gate-4.0/plugins/ANNIE/resources/gazetteer`. The file `lists.def` in the same directory is a list of lists that specifies which lists are actually used.

As an exercise, we will identify colour names in Sonnet 130. GATE provides a list of colour names, `colours.lst`, but it is not included in the standard version of `lists.def` so the gazetteer component does not normally annotate colours. In Figure 5.10, the standard gazetteer component has been replaced by `MyGazetteer` which uses a customized version of `lists.def` that includes an entry for `colours.lst`.

The gazetteer component creates Lookup annotations. Each Lookup annotation has a feature `majorType`, that is set to the string given in `lists.def`. For the colours list in Figure 5.10, the major type is specified as `colour` by the line `colours.lst:colour` in the middle column.

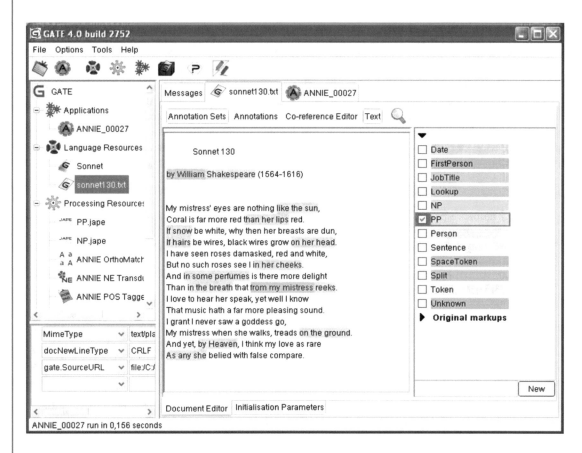

Figure 5.9: GATE: Prepositional Phrases annotated by JAPE rules.

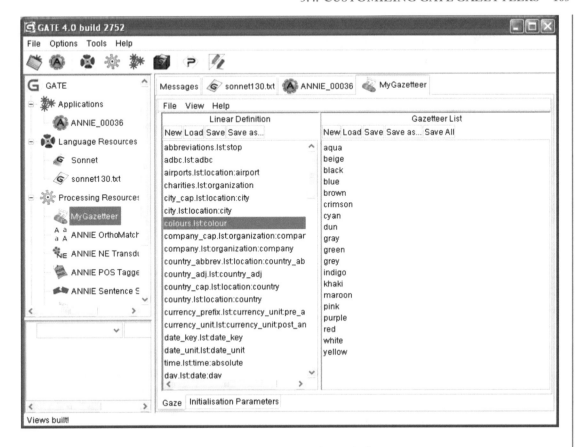

Figure 5.10: GATE: Customized gazetteer with colour list including *dun*.

The second level of customization decides which colours will be recognized. The lists are simple lists of names, one per line. The colours list `colours.lst` in the right-hand column in Figure 5.10 has been edited to include *dun*.

The third level of customization decides which named entities will have their own annotations in the Annotation Sets. This can be done by JAPE rules. The rule in Figure 5.11 matches Lookup annotations with major type `colour` and creates explicit `Colour` annotations.

When a JAPE transducer for this rule is added at the end of the processing pipeline, `Colour` annotations will be included in the Annotation Sets, as shown in Figure 5.12. Note that *dun*, which was added to the customized colours list, is identified as a colour, as well as *red, white* and *black*, which were in the colours list provided with GATE.

PRACTICAL WORK: CUSTOMIZING GATE GAZETTEERS

1. Customize the GATE gazetteer component so that it identifies colours in Sonnet 130, including *dun*, as shown in Figure 5.12.

```
Phase: Colour
Input: Lookup Token

Rule: Colour1
(
 {Lookup.majorType == colour}
)
:colour
-->
 :colour.Colour = {rule = "Colour1"}
```

Figure 5.11: GATE: JAPE rule for colour using gazetteer information.

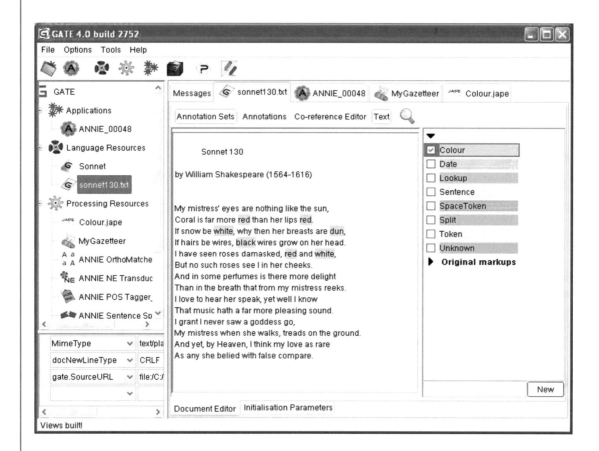

Figure 5.12: GATE: Identifying colours in Sonnet 130.

5.5   UIMA

Unstructured Information Management Architecture (UIMA) aims to provide a generalised framework for analyzing large amounts of text and other forms of unstructured information. The emphasis is on standards, interoperability and scalability. UIMA originated at IBM Research (`http://www.research.ibm.com/UIMA`) but is now open source. The Apache Software Foundation (`http://incubator.apache.org/uima/`) develops the software in Java, and the Organization for the Advancement of Structured Information Standards (OASIS) (`http://www.oasis-open.org/`) is responsible for defining standards and strategy.

In UIMA, *analysis engines* run *annotators*. Annotators can take the form of UIMA *wrappers* for existing NLP tools such as the OpenNLP tools, as described in Section 5.6. You can also develop new annotators in Java, as described in the tutorial by Nick Chase (Chase 2005). The simplest kind of Java annotator uses regular expressions to identify patterns in text. You can also install annotators from component repositories using PEAR, as described in Section 5.8.

An important architectural principle of UIMA is that all analysis engines operate on a standard data structure, the *Common Analysis System* (CAS) (Götz and Suhre 2004). The CAS includes both the text and the annotations. The text is referred to as the *Subject of Analysis* (SofA).

UIMA supports interoperability by using the XML Metadata Interchange (XMI) standard, which was described in Chapter 4. As we saw, in XMI the text is included in the CAS SofA as the `sofaString` attribute, and the annotations in the CAS have explicit XML namespace prefixes such as `<opennlp:Token>`.

Another important part of the UIMA architecture is the *type system*, which also supports interoperability. As we noted in Section 4.7, it is important to maintain a clear check on the content and type of the annotations. By checking the types of the annotations, it possible to make sure that annotations output from one component are the right types of annotations to be input to the next component. These checks can be done automatically by means of a type system. UIMA provides a ready-made type system `OpenNLPExampleTypes.xml` for use with the OpenNLP tools. We used this type system to view the XMI annotations in Section 4.6.

GETTING STARTED WITH UIMA AND ECLIPSE

Unlike GATE, UIMA does not have its own GUI because the Eclipse integrated development environment (IDE) is used as the GUI for UIMA (Figure 5.13). Both Eclipse and UIMA originated at IBM but are now open source. The Eclipse Foundation (`http://www.eclipse.org`) develops the Eclipse software in Java and is also responsible for standards and strategy. In the software industry, the Eclipse IDE is very popular, but it is not easy to get started with UIMA if you are unfamiliar with Eclipse, as it has its own learning curve. It is possible to use UIMA without Eclipse, as we did in Chapter 4 when we used UIMA Annotation Viewer to view XMI annotations. However, some UIMA tools do require Eclipse, such as UIMA Component Descriptor Editor.

Eclipse supports XML Metadata Interchange (XMI) format with Eclipse Modeling Framework (EMF). EMF was developed to support Unified Modeling Language (UML), and XMI is an XML interchange format for UML models. Note that EMF must be installed in Eclipse before using UIMA with Eclipse.

PRACTICAL WORK: INSTALLING ECLIPSE AND UIMA

1. Install Eclipse, following the instructions at `http://www.eclipse.org`.

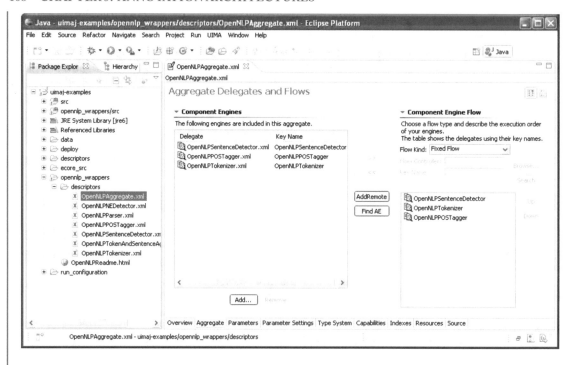

Figure 5.13: UIMA: Component flow in an aggregate analysis engine.

2. Install the appropriate version of EMF that matches the version of Eclipse.

3. Download UIMA from `http://incubator.apache.org/uima/`.

4. Install the UIMA Eclipse plugins, following the instructions in the UIMA *Overview and Setup* documentation.

5. Import the UIMA example code into an Eclipse project, as described in the UIMA *Overview and Setup* documentation.

5.6   UIMA WRAPPERS FOR OPENNLP TOOLS

The simplest way to get started using UIMA for linguistic annotation is to use the familiar OpenNLP tools with UIMA. The UIMA download includes a set of UIMA wrappers for OpenNLP tools. The OpenNLP tools are not included with UIMA: they must be installed separately before the UIMA wrappers can be used. The wrappers need to be compiled in UIMA. The practical work in this section assumes that you have already installed the OpenNLP tools and the OpenNLP models for English, which were used in Chapter 3.

RUNNING OPENNLP POS TAGGER IN UIMA

First, we use OpenNLP tools with their UIMA wrappers to do POS tagging. As we saw in Chapter 3, this requires a sequence of three OpenNLP components: sentence detector, tokenizer and POS tagger. Each component, when combined with its UIMA wrapper, is a UIMA annotator. An annotator used by itself is a *primitive analysis engine*. A sequence of annotators, combined to accomplish a larger task, is managed in UIMA by creating an *aggregate analysis engine*.

Both primitive and aggregate analysis engines are specified by *descriptors* which are XML files. You can edit the XML descriptor files by hand, but it is more convenient to use the graphical interface provided by the UIMA Component Descriptor Editor (CDE), shown in Figure 5.13.

The UIMA example code includes a descriptor file `OpenNLPAggregate.xml` for an aggregate analysis engine that includes OpenNLP sentence detector, OpenNLP tokenizer, and OpenNLP POS tagger. In Figure 5.13, this descriptor file has been opened for editing in CDE. The Aggregate tab has been selected, showing the three component annotators listed under Component Engines, and the order of their execution under Component Engine Flow.

Before this aggregate analysis engine can be run, its individual annotator components must be correctly set up. Each annotator requires the relevant OpenNLP model file for English. The locations of the model files are specified via a ModelFile parameter for each component. The parameter values can be edited in CDE by selecting the Parameter Settings tab, as shown in Figure 5.14. The ModelFile parameter has been selected under Configuration Parameters, and the value of the parameter has been edited under Values.

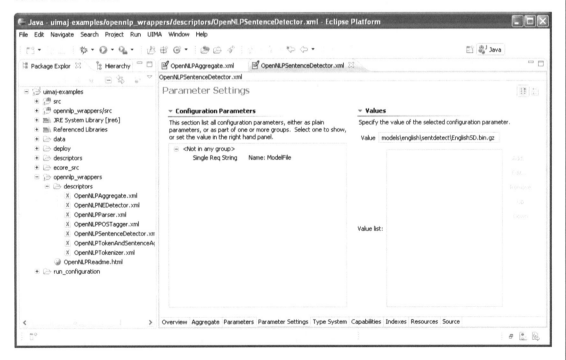

Figure 5.14: UIMA: Setting the ModelFile parameter for Sentence Detector.

PRACTICAL WORK: INSTALLING OPENNLP TOOLS IN UIMA

1. In Eclipse, compile the UIMA wrappers for OpenNLP. Detailed instructions are given in the file `OpenNLPReadme.html` in the `opennlp_wrappers` subdirectory of the UIMA example code.

2. In Eclipse, run Component Descriptor Editor (CDE) on the descriptor file `OpenNLPSentenceDetector.xml` in the `opennlp_wrappers/descriptors` subdirectory. Edit the value of the ModelFile parameter to the location where the OpenNLP model for English sentence detector is installed. This step is shown in Figure 5.14.

3. Similarly, run CDE on `OpenNLPTokenizer.xml` and `OpenNLPPOSTagger.xml` to edit the values of the ModelFile parameters to the correct locations.

PRACTICAL WORK: RUNNING OPENNLP POS TAGGER IN UIMA

1. Launch UIMA Document Analyzer, as shown in Figure 5.15. From Eclipse this is done using Run or Open Run Dialog.

2. In UIMA Document Analyzer, analyze `sonnet130.txt`. Run the aggregate analysis engine using the descriptor `OpenNLPAggregate.xml`.

3. The results should be like Figure 5.16. We noted in Chapter 4 that *dun* is incorrectly tagged as VBN by OpenNLP tagger, and saw how to use WordFreak to edit the POS tags and how to transform the annotations to XMI format.

CONFIGURING COMPONENTS IN UIMA

In UIMA, components are configured by combining them in aggregate analysis engines. The aggregate analysis engine shown in Figure 5.13 combines OpenNLP sentence detector, OpenNLP tokenizer, and OpenNLP POS tagger. We will add OpenNLP parser to the aggregate.

PRACTICAL WORK: CONFIGURING OPENNLP PARSER IN UIMA

1. Run Component Descriptor Editor (CDE) on `OpenNLPParser.xml` in the `opennlp_wrappers/descriptors` subdirectory. In the Parameter Settings tab, set the ModelFile parameter to the correct location.

2. Using CDE, add OpenNLP parser to the aggregate analysis engine. This is shown in Figure 5.17.

PRACTICAL WORK: RUNNING OPENNLP PARSER IN UIMA

1. Run the new aggregate analysis engine in UIMA Document Analyzer.

2. The results should be similar to Figure 5.18.

The language of Shakespeare's sonnets is difficult to parse, even for humans. The OpenNLP parser has made a good attempt, but Figure 5.18 highlights one point where we would choose a different analysis. The parser correctly parses *in her cheeks* as a prepositional phrase (PP), but it includes this PP in a noun phrase (NP) *I in her cheeks*. This is one possibility, with the meaning *I who am in her cheeks*, but this is relatively unlikely even in a romantic poem.

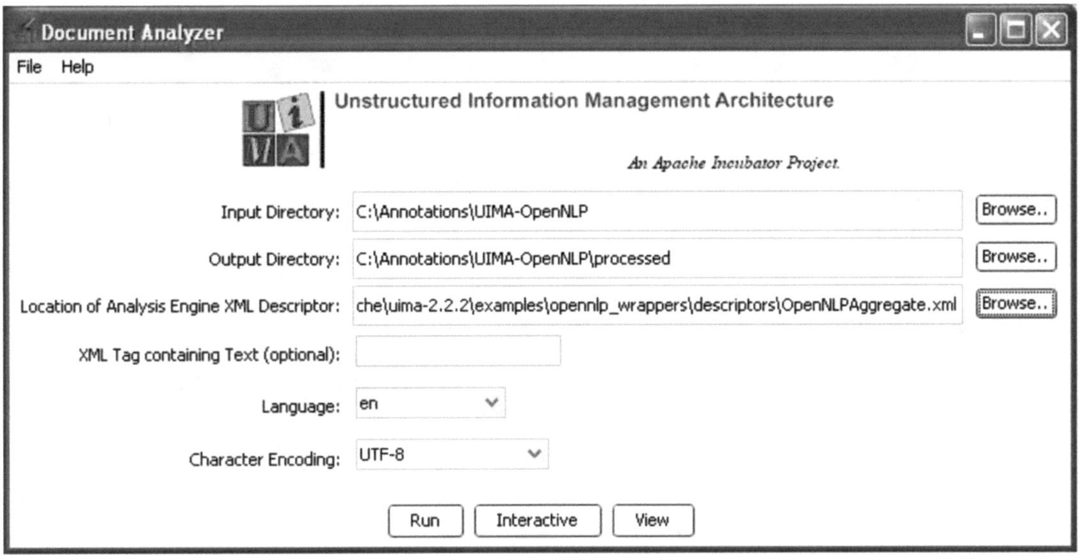

Figure 5.15: UIMA: Running OpenNLP POS tagger.

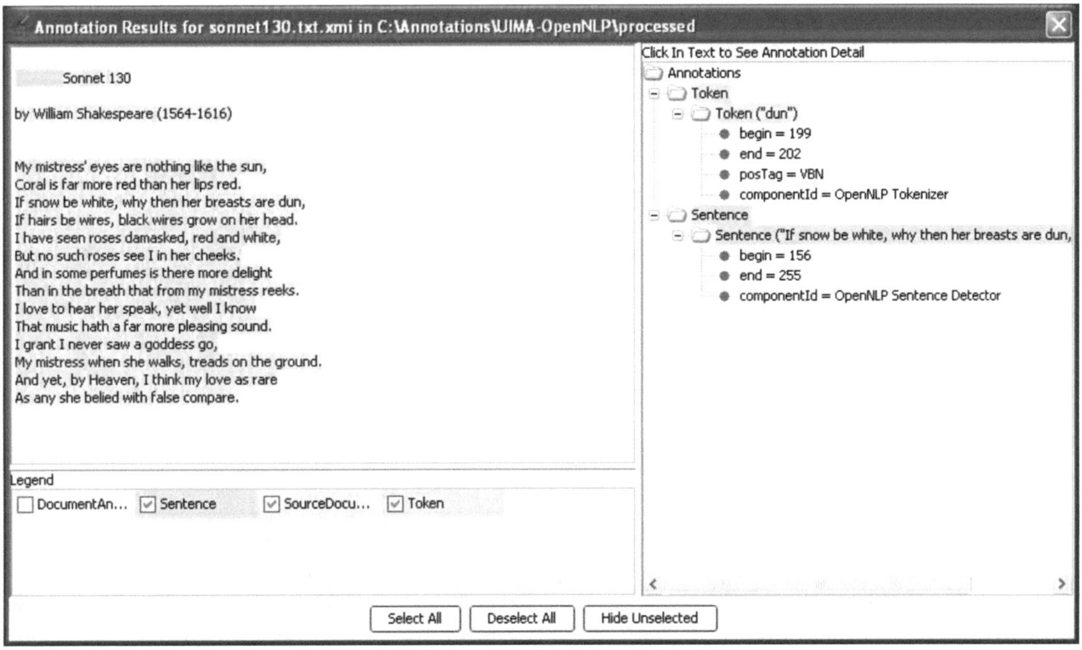

Figure 5.16: UIMA Annotation Viewer showing *dun* tagged VBN by OpenNLP.

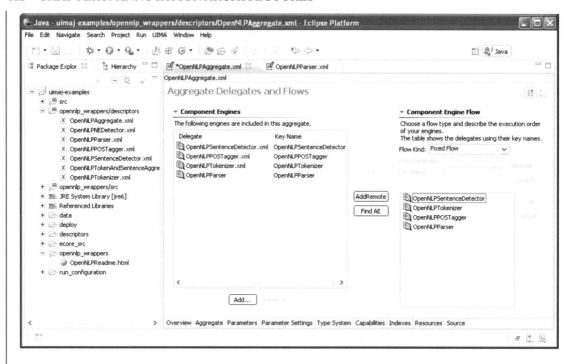

Figure 5.17: UIMA: Adding OpenNLP parser to an aggregate analysis engine.

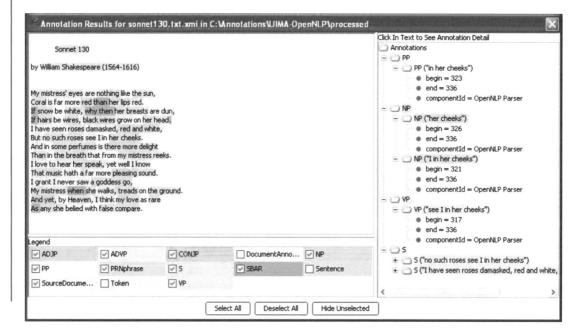

Figure 5.18: UIMA: Sonnet 130 parsed by OpenNLP parser.

As a consequence, the sentence (S) *no such roses see I in her cheeks* would mean *I who am in her cheeks see no such roses*. A better analysis would keep the NP *I* and the PP *in her cheeks* separate, so the PP can be attached either to the verb *see*, with the meaning *I see in her cheeks no such roses*, or to the NP *no such roses*, with the meaning *I see no such roses that are in her cheeks*.

The Stanford parser does well here. It attaches the PP *in her cheeks* to the verb *see*, as shown in Figure 3.10 in Chapter 3.

5.7   ANNOTATIONS WITH REGULAR EXPRESSIONS

A set of additional annotation tools is available as a separate *Addons* download from the UIMA website. The Addons download includes a whitespace tokenizer, an HMM part-of-speech tagger, a regular expression annotator, and a dictionary annotator. These tools can be combined to build applications that do named entity recognition. We start with the tokenizer and tagger, and then describe the regular expression annotator in this section. The dictionary annotator is described in Section 5.8.

UIMA ADDONS: TOKENIZER AND TAGGER

Figure 5.19 shows one way to set up the annotators from the Addons download, using a standard directory structure that is recommended for UIMA projects. This directory structure is also used by PEAR archives.

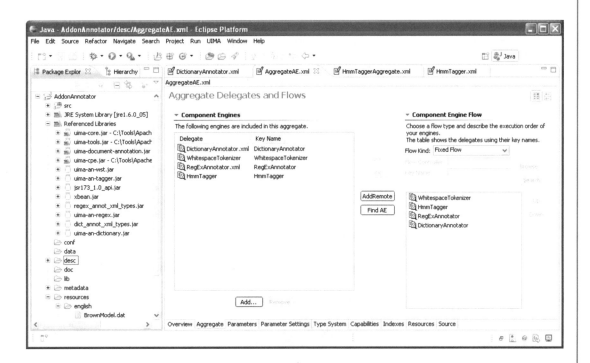

Figure 5.19: UIMA Addons: Aggregate analysis engine.

The descriptors are in the `desc` folder. The jar files are in the `lib` folder, but Eclipse does not show them in `lib`, as they have also been added to the list of Referenced Libraries. The statistical model `BrownModel.dat` is in the `resources/english` subfolder. This model was trained on the Brown corpus. The descriptor `HmmTagger.xml` has been edited in CDE to specify the location of the model folder.

The aggregate analysis engine can be run in UIMA Document Analyzer to tokenize and tag texts. The result for Sonnet 130 is shown in Figure 5.20. Note that *dun* is incorrectly tagged nn (noun), the same error as the GATE tagger. The POS tag is lower case because the Brown corpus uses lower case tags.

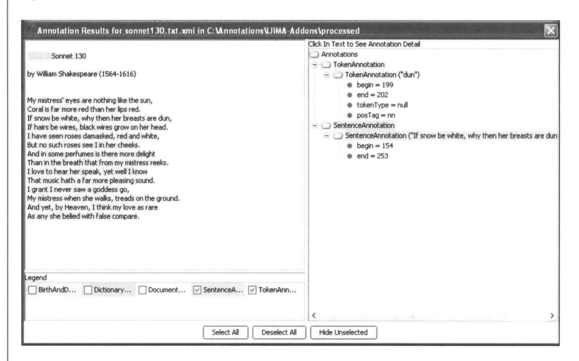

Figure 5.20: UIMA Addons: Sonnet 130 tagged by HMM Tagger.

UIMA ADDONS: REGULAR EXPRESSION ANNOTATOR

The Addons download also includes a regular expression annotator. This can be used to identify named entities that conform to restricted patterns, such as telephone numbers, email addresses, and URLs. The tutorial by Nick Chase (Chase 2005) shows Java programmers how to develop a UIMA annotator to recognize room numbers using regular expressions in Java. The importance of the regular expression annotator in the Addons download is that it enables non-programmers to create, and customize, this kind of annotator.

The regular expressions are specified and customized in a *concepts file* (Figure 5.21). In the project setup shown in Figure 5.19 the concepts file `author-concepts.xml` is in the `resources` folder. The XML schema `concepts.xsd` is also in the `resources` folder. The descriptor `RegExAnnotator.xml`

Figure 5.21: UIMA Addons: Regular Expression Annotator concepts file.

has been edited in CDE to specify the location of the concepts file in the Parameter Settings tab, and to specify the input and output annotation types in the Capabilities tab.

The concepts file `author-concepts.xml` shown in Figure 5.21 is a customized version of `concepts.xml` from the download. The customized regular expression in `<rules>` will match any sequence of left parenthesis, year, hyphen, year, right parenthesis, and will also return the values of the two years in the variables $1 and $2, following standard practice with regular expressions. The `<createAnnotations>` part of the concepts file creates a `<BirthAndDeath>` annotation, and sets two features `yearOfBirth` and `yearOfDeath` to the actual values in $1 and $2. The result for Sonnet 130 is shown in Figure 5.22.

5.8   CUSTOMIZING UIMA DICTIONARIES

In UIMA, dictionary annotators support named entity recognition in a similar way to the use of gazetteers in GATE. As an exercise, we will use the dictionary annotator to identify colour names in Sonnet 130, as we did with GATE gazetteers in Section 5.4.

UIMA ADDONS: DICTIONARY ANNOTATOR

The code for dictionary annotators is provided in the Addons download. In the project setup shown in Figure 5.19 the dictionary file `color-dictionary.xml` is in the `resources` folder. This is a customized version of `dictionary.xml` from the download. The XML schema `dictionary.xsd` is also in the

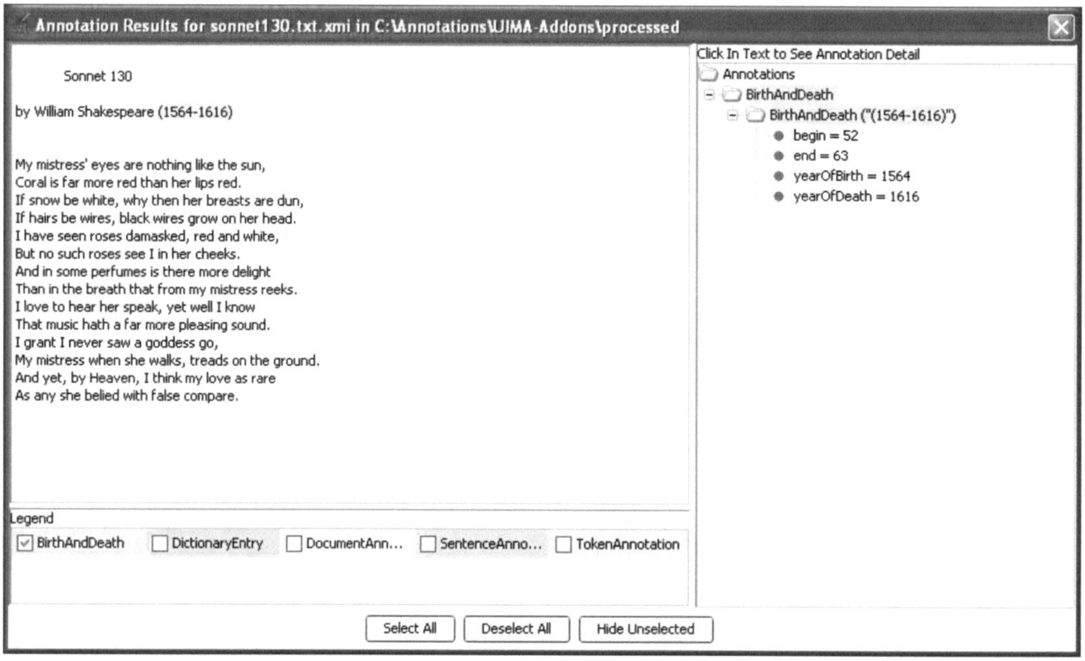

Figure 5.22: UIMA RegEx Annotator: Identifying years of birth and death.

resources folder. The descriptor `DictionaryAnnotator.xml` has been edited in CDE to specify the location of the dictionary file in the Parameter Settings tab, and to specify the input and output annotation types in the Capabilities tab.

CUSTOMIZING THE DICTIONARY FILE

The dictionary file `color-dictionary.xml` lists the colours to be identified, as shown in Figure 5.23. Each colour name to be recognized is specified as the value of a `<key>` element in an `<entry>` in the list of `<entries>`.

The colour names in Figure 5.23 are copied from `colours.lst`, the GATE gazetteer that we used in Section 5.4. The colour *dun* has been added to show how the list can be customized. Clearly, other name lists can easily be converted to this format for use in named entity recognition. The XML format means that the name lists are not quite as easy to customize as the plain text lists used by GATE, but it also offers possibilities for validating the lists using either the standard XML schema provided in the download, or using a customized schema to enforce more specific restrictions on the entries.

The aggregate analysis engine specified by the descriptor `AggregateAE.xml` runs the whitespace tokenizer followed by the dictionary annotator. When the aggregate analysis engine is run on Sonnet 130, the colours mentioned in the sonnet (including *dun*) are identified as shown in Figure 5.24. The results are the same as in Section 5.4 with the customized GATE gazetteer.

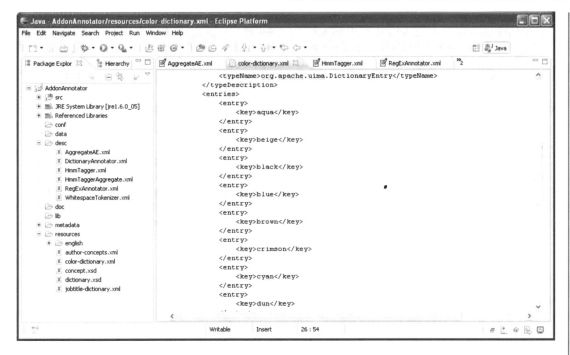

Figure 5.23: UIMA Dictionary Annotator: `color-dictionary.xml`.

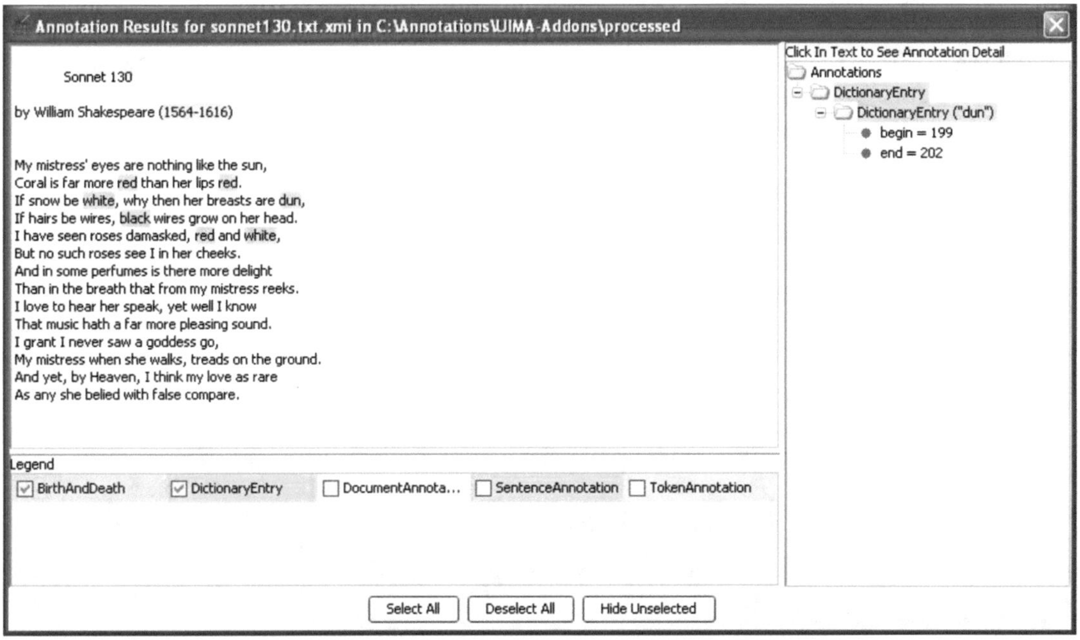

Figure 5.24: UIMA Dictionary Annotator: Identifying colours in Sonnet 130.

PEAR FILES

The components of the Addons download are examples of components that have been packaged as UIMA PEAR files. PEAR (Processing Engine Archive) is a standard format for saving, distributing, and deploying UIMA components. The PEAR directory structure, which was shown in Section 5.7, is recommended for use in UIMA projects.

PEAR format supports a particularly easy way to install components using the UIMA PEAR Installer. This is described in the *PEAR Installer User's Guide* in the UIMA documentation.

COMPONENT REPOSITORIES

UIMA annotators and other components can be downloaded from component repositories on the web. Components are usually available from repositories in PEAR format for ease of installation.

There is a general UIMA component repository at CMU (Carnegie Mellon University) (http://uima.lti.cs.cmu.edu). Another component repository, with a focus on bioinformatics, is JCoRe (Hahn et al. 2008) at Jena University Language and Information Engineering Lab (http://www.julielab.de).

5.9   FURTHER READING

Both GATE and UIMA have their own extensive on-line documentation.

- GATE: See the *GATE User Guide* (Cunningham et al. 2009).

- UIMA: See *UIMA manuals and Guides* at
  http://incubator.apache.org/uima/documentation.html.

- UIMA's IBM origins: See (Ferrucci and Lally 2004), (Götz and Suhre 2004).

- UIMA component repositories: See http://uima.lti.cs.cmu.edu (CMU) and http://www.julielab.de (Jena).

C H A P T E R   6

Text Analytics

The term *text analytics* refers to a subfield of information technology that deals with applications, systems and services that do some kind of analysis of texts in order to extract information from them.

The basic techniques for text analytics were developed in the 1990's by participants in the series of Message Understanding Conferences (`http://www.muc.saic.com`). The MUC conferences defined three challenges: named entity recognition, coreference resolution, and information extraction. By the time of MUC-7 in 1998 good progress had been made in named entity recognition, with less progress in coreference and information extraction (Chinchor 1998).

After 1998, work on fundamental techniques for text analytics continued in the series of Computational Natural Language Learning (CoNLL) conferences (`http://ifarm.nl/signll/conll/`). These conferences made good progress by concentrating on specific shared tasks, for example chunking in 2000, named entity recognition in 2002 and 2003, semantic role labeling in 2004 and 2005.

This chapter describes tools and techniques for text analytics. Section 6.1 reviews tools, focussing on those tools that are freely available. The rest of the chapter illustrates techniques and applications.

As named entity recognition is fundamental, we describe more than one approach. Section 6.2 describes two implementations of gazetteer-based entity recognition, while Section 6.3 shows how to train statistical models. Section 6.4 illustrates the challenges of coreference resolution, which is still a difficult field. Section 6.5 shows how to use a commercial tool, IBM LanguageWare Resource Workbench, to create UIMA annotators for information extraction.

Text analytics applications are generally based on finding effective ways to exploit information extraction results. These include text data mining and semantic search, described in Section 6.6. Finally, some new directions in text analytics are mentioned in Section 6.7.

6.1   TEXT ANALYTICS TOOLS

We only consider freely-available Java tools, that are useful for programmers developing text analytics applications in Java. NLTK (`http://nltk.org`) is an excellent Python NLP toolkit that is suitable for research and teaching.

OPEN SOURCE TOOLS

OpenNLP provides a set of tools for NLP tasks, and leaves the design of text analytics applications to the application developer. The tools cover all the main tasks, as we saw in Chapter 3: sentence detection, tokenization, POS tagging, phrase chunking, sentence parsing, named entity recognition and coreference resolution. The tools are easy to use as plugins in Java applications.

The Stanford NLP tools are not a comprehensive toolkit like OpenNLP, rather they specialize in specific tasks: tagging, parsing, and named entity recognition. As they are free-standing tools with their own GUIs, they are less easy to use as plugins in text analytics applications than the OpenNLP tools.

GATE is an architecture, as we saw in Chapter 5, but it also comes with an extensive toolkit and a ready-made text analytics application, the ANNIE information extraction system. This includes a sentence splitter, tokenizer, POS tagger, gazetteer lookup, and named entity recognizer. Many other tools can easily be added to the pipeline, as we saw in Section 5.2. In addition to the tools for basic NLP tasks, GATE also provides support for application development in other ways. For example, GATE provides machine learning tools, and also supports the integration of NLP with ontologies.

UIMA is an architecture rather than a toolkit, as we saw in Chapter 5, but the OpenNLP wrappers and the ready-made annotators in the Addons download provide a useful set of tools. An overview of building text analytics applications with UIMA is given by (Ferrucci and Lally 2004). The tutorial by Nick Chase (Chase 2005) shows in detail how to create a Java application with UIMA.

In addition to these NLP tools, there are other open source Java tools that are very useful when building text analytics applications. These include Lucene (Gospodnetić and Hatcher 2004) for indexing and searching, and Weka (Witten and Frank 2005) for machine learning and data mining.

COMMERCIAL TOOLS

Up-to-date information on commercial text analytics tools can be found from the Annual Text Analytics Summits (http://www.textanalyticsnews.com). Some commercial tools offer royalty-free research licenses or free temporary download for evaluation purposes.

LingPipe (http://alias-i.com/lingpipe) is a commercial text analytics toolkit licensed by Alias-i (Figure 6.1). A royalty-free license is available for research use. The LingPipe website includes detailed tutorials on text analytics tasks such as topic classification, named entity recognition, spelling

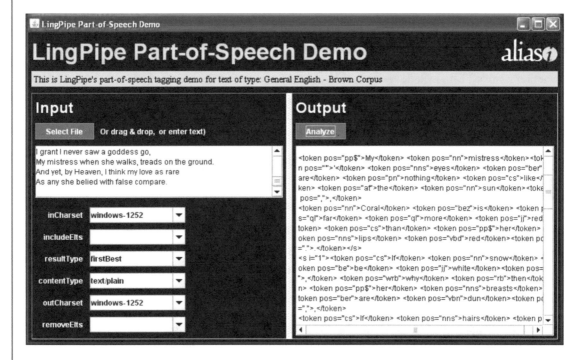

Figure 6.1: Tokens and tags in LingPipe part-of-speech demo.

correction, and sentiment analysis. The tutorials are intended for Java programmers who wish to develop text analytics applications using LingPipe's Java API.

Figure 6.1 shows Sonnet 130 tagged in the LingPipe part-of-speech demo. In the demo, in-line annotations are used, not stand-off annotations. Note that *dun* is tagged VBN, the same error as OpenNLP tagger.

LanguageWare Resource Workbench (http://www.alphaworks.ibm.com/tech/lrw) is a commercial text analytics tool licensed by IBM. The product can be downloaded free of charge for a fixed period for evaluation purposes.

LanguageWare Resource Workbench is integrated with Eclipse and UIMA, which is no surprise as they also originated at IBM. A significant advantage of this integration is that annotators developed with LanguageWare Resource Workbench can be deployed with PEAR directly in UIMA applications.

The *Getting Started Guide* (IBM 2008) describes how to create dictionaries, rules and annotators. We give examples of entity recognition and information extraction using LanguageWare Resource Workbench in Section 6.5.

Figure 6.2 shows Sonnet 130 tagged by LanguageWare Resource Workbench. Note that *dun* is

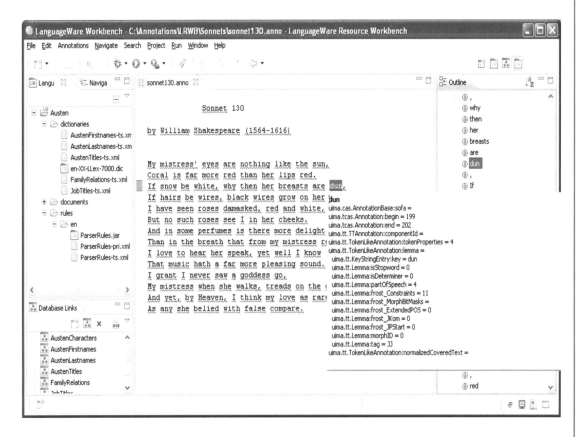

Figure 6.2: Tokens and tags in LanguageWare Resources Workbench.

correctly tagged as an adjective (JJ). Of all the tools we have described (OpenNLP, GATE, UIMA Addons, LingPipe), this is the only one whose tagger got this right.

AN EXAMPLE TEXT

For the examples in this chapter, we will use Jane Austen's *Northanger Abbey*. Shakespeare's sonnets are too short to serve as realistic example texts, and the language of the sonnets is far too difficult for our parsers. By contrast, *Northanger Abbey* is long enough to be realistic without being too long, and the language is a model of clarity. A public domain version of the novel is available from Project Gutenberg (`http://www.gutenberg.org`).

PRACTICAL WORK: DOWNLOAD *NORTHANGER ABBEY*

1. Download the plain text file of *Northanger Abbey* from Project Gutenberg.

2. Edit the file to remove the explanatory matter at the start and end, which is not part of the text of the novel.

3. Save the edited file as `nabbey.txt` for use in the practical work.

CONCORDANCES

Some forms of text analysis require very little preliminary annotation. For example, it is possible to make a concordance of the text as soon as tokenization has been done. A concordance is used in corpus linguistics to study the usage of words, by showing the surrounding words immediately before and after a given word in actual sentences from a particular text. WordFreak includes a useful concordance tool.

PRACTICAL WORK: CONCORDANCE IN WORDFREAK

1. Load `nabbey.txt` into WordFreak and do tokenization.

2. Select Viewer → Concordance. Depending on processing power, creating the concordance may take some time.

3. Select Edit → Find, and input *father*. Figure 6.3 shows the results.

6.2   NAMED ENTITY RECOGNITION

Named entity recognition is the foundation of text analytics. Of the three tasks identified by the MUC conferences (named entity recognition, coreference resolution, and information extraction), named entity recognition is a prerequisite for the other two. Successful information extraction depends on accurate named entity recognition.

To illustrate named entity recognition, we set ourselves the task of finding job titles in *Northanger Abbey*. As it is fundamental, we present more than one approach. This section describes a rule-based approach, first using GATE and then using UIMA. The GATE implementation does gazetteer lookup, refined with JAPE rules. The UIMA implementation uses a customized dictionary annotator. Section 6.3 describes a statistical approach to the same task, implemented by training an OpenNLP maximum entropy model for job titles.

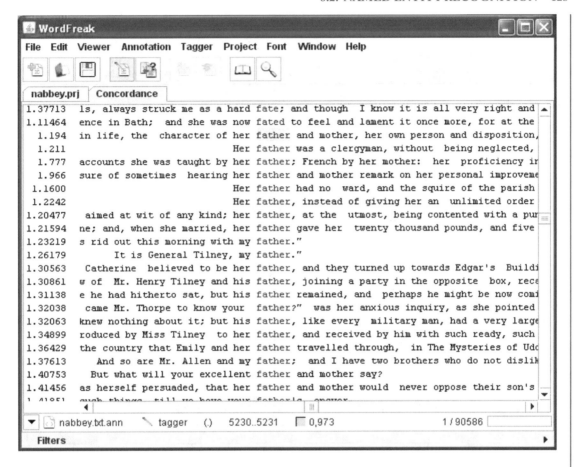

Figure 6.3: Concordance for *Northanger Abbey* in WordFreak.

GATE GAZETTEER FOR JOB TITLES

Figure 6.4 shows the result of running ANNIE on *Northanger Abbey*. Using the standard ANNIE gazetteer list of job titles, GATE has found 264 job titles.

Many of the items found are occurrences of *father*. Although *father* can be a job title for a priest, as in G. K. Chesterton's *Father Brown Stories*, in Jane Austen's *Northanger Abbey* it is used consistently as a family relationship, not as a job title. This can be seen with a concordance, as shown in Figure 6.3.

In information retrieval terminology, items that are found or selected are called *positives*, and items that are selected, but are not correct examples of the thing being looked for, are called *false positives*. In *Northanger Abbey*, none the occurrences of *father* are job titles, so they are false positives. The simplest way to avoid marking *father* as a job title is to remove it from the gazetteer list. However, there is a useful technique using JAPE rules that is worth knowing, that we describe in the next section.

Apart from *father*, many others in the 264 selected items are false positives. For example, in Figure 6.5, GATE has marked *judge* as a job title, but in this case it is a verb (*to judge*). In general, only

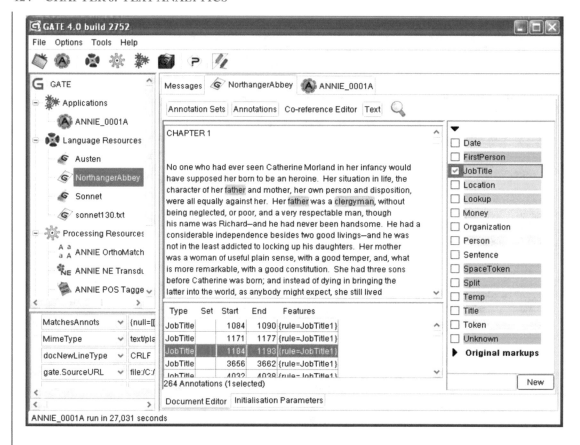

Figure 6.4: GATE: job titles in *Northanger Abbey*, including *father*.

nouns are job titles, not verbs. In order to reduce the number of false positives, POS tags should be checked as well as gazetteer lists. This is an example of the principle that good annotations support good analysis. Job title analysis can be done simply by using gazetteer lists, but if POS tag annotations are done first, they can be used to improve the precision of the job title analysis.

GATE GAZETTEER PLUS JAPE RULES

There is no way to check for negative conditions in JAPE rules, so we cannot check directly that a token is not equal to *father*. However, rule priorities can be used to achieve the same effect.

The rules in Figure 6.6 apply to items that have already been annotated as `JobTitle` by the gazetteer lookup component. They add a new annotation `NounJobTitle` to those items that are nouns but are not *father*.

The first rule checks if a `JobTitle` is the string *father*. If so, it does nothing; it does not create a `NounJobTitle` annotation for this span. Note that it is not sufficient to check the context for a preceding possessive pronoun: *her father* is not a job title, but *her doctor* is, so the actual string must be checked.

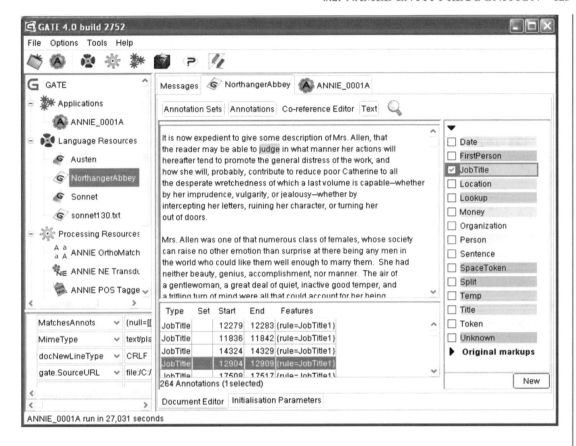

Figure 6.5: GATE job titles: a false positive.

The second rule checks if a `JobTitle` is also a noun (NN). If so, it creates a new `NounJobTitle` annotation for this span. Otherwise, it does not. The first rule has a higher priority than the second rule, so if the first rule matches, then the second rule will not match. This requires the control option to be `appelt`.

Figure 6.7 shows the result of running ANNIE plus the JAPE transducer with the rules in Figure 6.6. Now *clergyman* is marked as *NounJobTitle*, but *father* is not. Using the standard ANNIE gazetteer list of job titles, GATE found 264 job titles in *Northanger Abbey*, as shown in Figure 6.4. By using the standard job titles gazetteer list in combination with the JAPE rules, the number of job titles found is reduced to 132.

PRECISION AND RECALL

In information retrieval, finding most of the things you are looking for is high *recall*. Finding them without getting many false positives is high *precision*.

```
Phase: NE
Input: Token JobTitle
Options: control = appelt

Rule: NotFather
Priority: 20
(
  {JobTitle, Token.category == "NN", Token.string == "father"}
):father
-->
  {}

Rule: NounJobTitle
Priority: 5
(
  {JobTitle, Token.category == "NN"}
):noun
-->
  :noun.NounJobTitle = {rule = "NounJobTitle"}
```

Figure 6.6: GATE: JAPE rules for job titles using POS information.

To calculate recall, divide the number of true positives that you found by the total number of target items (true positives plus *false negatives*: false negatives are the target items that you missed). To calculate precision, divide the true positives by the total positives (true positives plus false positives).

In Chapter 1 of *Northanger Abbey*, the original ANNIE gazetteer found 5 true positives (*clergyman, music-master, lord, baronet, squire*) and 9 false positives (*father* 5 times, *elder, corporal, hero, chief*). This gives recall = 5/5 = 100% and precision = 5/14 = 36%.

The aim of the rules in Figure 6.6 is to maintain the same high recall while increasing the precision by reducing the number of false positives. As the total number of positives was reduced from 264 in Figure 6.5 to 132 in Figure 6.7, the rules have clearly had an impact. However, it turns out that *music-master* was incorrectly tagged JJ (adjective), so it becomes a false negative. Using the rules, in Chapter 1 recall = 4/5 = 80% and precision = 4/7 = 57%.

UIMA DICTIONARY FOR JOB TITLES

We now show how the same rule-based approach to named entity recognition that we used with GATE can also be implemented with UIMA. First, we need a UIMA dictionary for job titles. The GATE gazetteer list for job titles can easily be converted to a UIMA dictionary file, in the same way as the gazetteer list for colours, described in Chapter 5, Section 5.8. Naturally, the results of using a UIMA dictionary annotator with such a dictionary will be the same as for GATE. Both *father* and *clergyman* will be found by the annotator, but the dictionary can easily be customized by removing *father*.

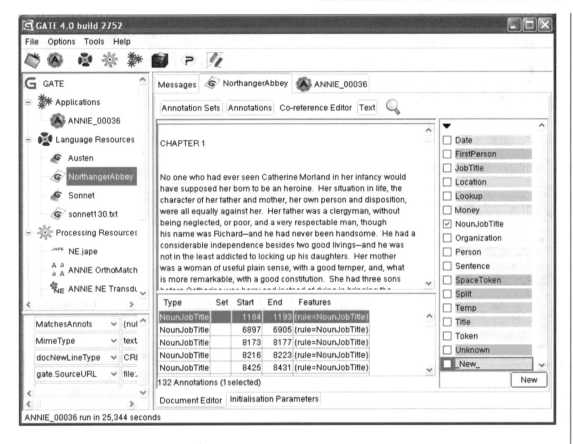

Figure 6.7: GATE job titles: *clergyman* and not *father*.

Figure 6.8 shows both false and true positives. UIMA has marked *judge*, *usher* and *maid* as job titles, but *judge* and *usher* are false positives. Only *maid*, which is a noun, is a true positive here. Both *to judge* and *to usher* are verbs, and as we already remarked, only nouns are job titles, not verbs. In order to reduce the number of false positives, POS tags should be checked as well as dictionary lists.

UIMA DICTIONARY WITH CONDITIONS

With UIMA dictionary annotator, conditions can be specified to control whether dictionary entries are matched or not. This is done in the annotator's XML descriptor. Figure 6.9 shows the `<configurationParameterSettings>` element in the descriptor.

The first `<nameValuePair>` element says that the name of the dictionary file is `jobtitle-dictionary.xml`. The second `<nameValuePair>` says that `<InputMatchType>` is `TokenAnnotation`, in other words this annotator only processes tokenized tokens. The next three `<nameValuePair>` elements specify the condition for matching. Taken together, they say that a match

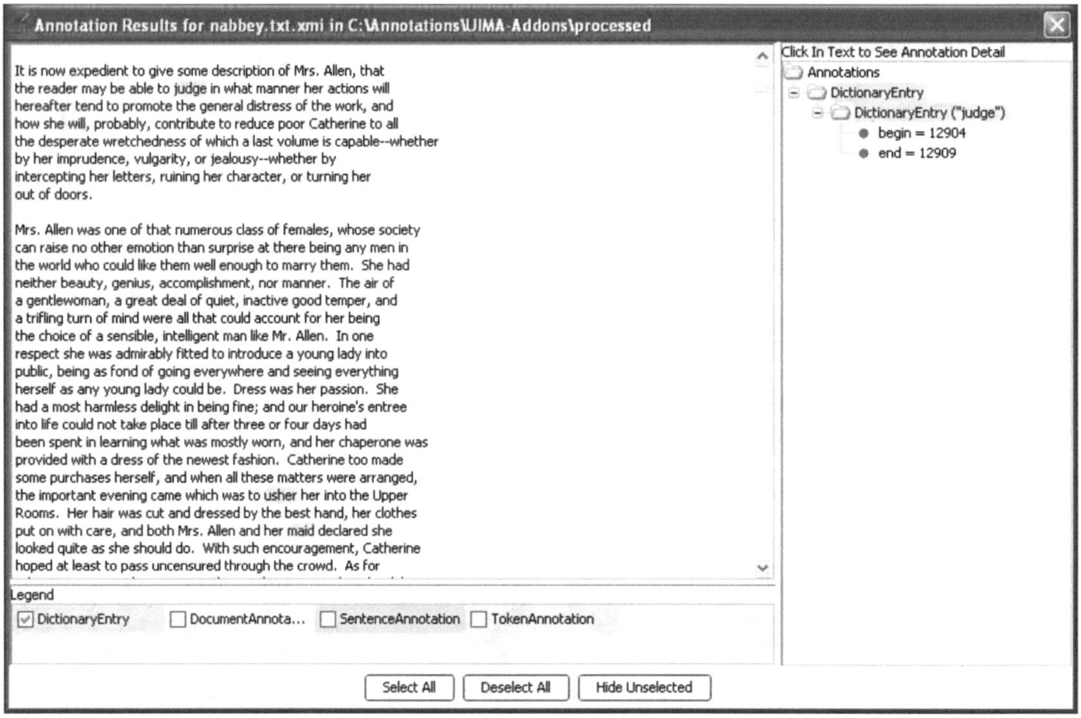

Figure 6.8: UIMA job titles: false positives and a true positive.

is found only if a token's `posTag` equals "nn" (noun). The POS tag is lowercase because this annotator is used with the UIMA Addons HMM tagger, which was trained with the Brown Corpus (see Section 5.7).

When these conditions are added to the dictionary annotator the number of false positives is greatly reduced. Compare Figure 6.8 (without the conditions) and Figure 6.10 (with the conditions). With the conditions, UIMA has marked only *maid* as a job title. Both *judge* and *usher* are unmatched. In information retrieval terms, they are now *true negatives*.

6.3 TRAINING STATISTICAL MODELS

This section describes a statistical approach to named entity recognition. The task is the same: to find job titles in *Northanger Abbey*. Section 3.6 in Chapter 3 showed how to use OpenNLP name finder to do named entity recognition with the ready-made models that you can download from the OpenNLP website. As there is no ready-made model for job titles, we need to train a new model.

There is very little documentation about how to train new models. The OpenNLP README file contains a brief paragraph about it, but no details or examples. The OpenNLP discussion forum (https://sourceforge.net/forum/forum.php?forum_id=9943) includes a number of related questions and helpful answers. As there is so little documentation, we illustrate here the basic steps required for training a new model.

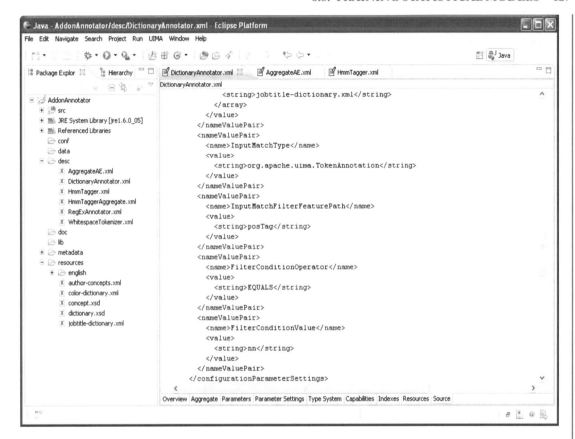

Figure 6.9: UIMA job titles dictionary: specifying conditions.

TESTING A MODEL

OpenNLP name finder can find names for different types of entities, using a separate model for each type. There are 7 ready-made models: person, location, organization, date, time, money, percentage. The namefinder script in Chapter 3 loads all the models that are in the models directory. When doing repeated cycles of training and testing, loading several models is relatively slow. It's quicker to train and test one model at a time.

PRACTICAL WORK: TESTING ONE MODEL

1. The script in Figure 6.11 runs the OpenNLP name finder, loading only the models that are in the current directory. This speeds up testing.

2. Copy the file person.bin.gz from the OpenNLP models directory to your testing directory. This is the ready-made model for person names.

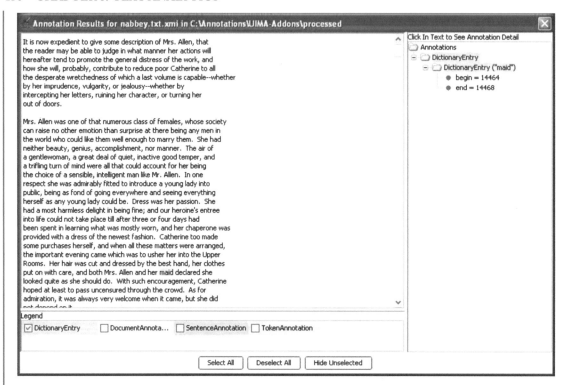

Figure 6.10: UIMA job titles: true negatives and a true positive.

3. Use the script like this to do find person names in *Northanger Abbey*:
   `./opennlp-nametester.sh <nabbey.txt >nabbey-persons.txt &`.
   It annotates a few names, such as `<person>Catherine</person>`.

TRAINING A NEW MODEL

In principle, we can train models to find anything we want. Training is done with a training file. An example is shown in Figure 6.12.

In the training file, examples of the things we want to find are marked with `<START>` and `<END>` tags. Note that these are not valid XML tags: this is just a simple way of marking the examples. The training file is plain text, not XML. The format of the training file should be like an OpenNLP tokenized file, with sentences separated by newlines and tokens separated by spaces.

An example must occur at least 5 times to pass the threshold for inclusion in the model. A naive approach, aiming to keep the training file short, is to use only the sentences that contain an example and repeat each sentence 5 times, as in Figure 6.12.

```
#!/bin/sh
# Shell script to run OpenNLP-1.3.0 name finder
# using only models in the current directory
# G. Wilcock 21.11.2007
#
# Usage: ./opennlp-nametester.sh < input.txt > namesfound.txt

OPENNLP_HOME=~gwilcock/Tools/opennlp-1.3.0
export OPENNLP_HOME

CLASSPATH=.:\
$OPENNLP_HOME/lib/opennlp-tools-1.3.0.jar:\
$OPENNLP_HOME/lib/maxent-2.4.0.jar:\
$OPENNLP_HOME/lib/trove.jar
export CLASSPATH

java opennlp.tools.lang.english.SentenceDetector \
 $OPENNLP_HOME/models/english/sentdetect/EnglishSD.bin.gz |
java -Xmx1024m opennlp.tools.lang.english.NameFinder \
 *.bin.gz
```

Figure 6.11: `opennlp-nametester.sh`: A script to test new models.

PRACTICAL WORK: TRAINING A JOB TITLE MODEL

1. The script in Figure 6.13 runs the OpenNLP Java class `NameFinderME` to train maximum entropy models (ME is Maximum Entropy).

2. Train a job title model (jobtitle.bin.gz) with the training file like this:
   `./opennlp-nametrainer.sh train-jobtitles.txt jobtitle.bin.gz &`.

3. Test the person model and job title model with the test file (nabbey.txt):
   `./opennlp-nametester <nabby.txt >person-job-names.txt &`.
   With these two models, name finder finds both persons and job titles.

However, this naive approach does not work. In the short training file the relative frequency of job title examples is too high. The resulting model causes name finder to find too many false positives, as shown in Figure 6.14.

It is necessary to include sufficient examples that do not contain job titles: examples of true negatives. To develop a serious model, training files with large numbers of examples need to be used.

STATISTICAL MODEL VS. GAZETTEER LIST

An advantage of using a statistical model rather than a gazetteer list is that new or otherwise unknown job titles can be recognized, even though they are not in the list. Given the example *Her father was a*

Her father was a <START> clergyman <END> , without being neglected ,
or poor , and a very respectable man , though his name was Richard
-- and he had never been handsome .
Her father was a <START> clergyman <END> , without being neglected ,
or poor , and a very respectable man , though his name was Richard
-- and he had never been handsome .
Her father was a <START> clergyman <END> , without being neglected ,
or poor , and a very respectable man , though his name was Richard
-- and he had never been handsome .
Her father was a <START> clergyman <END> , without being neglected ,
or poor , and a very respectable man , though his name was Richard
-- and he had never been handsome .
Her father was a <START> clergyman <END> , without being neglected ,
or poor , and a very respectable man , though his name was Richard
-- and he had never been handsome .
There was not one <START> lord <END> in the neighbourhood ;
 no -- not even a <START> baronet <END> .
There was not one <START> lord <END> in the neighbourhood ;
 no -- not even a <START> baronet <END> .
There was not one <START> lord <END> in the neighbourhood ;
 no -- not even a <START> baronet <END> .
There was not one <START> lord <END> in the neighbourhood ;
 no -- not even a <START> baronet <END> .
There was not one <START> lord <END> in the neighbourhood ;
 no -- not even a <START> baronet <END> .
Her father had no ward , and the <START> squire <END> of the parish
no children .
Her father had no ward , and the <START> squire <END> of the parish
no children .
Her father had no ward , and the <START> squire <END> of the parish
no children .
Her father had no ward , and the <START> squire <END> of the parish
no children .
Her father had no ward , and the <START> squire <END> of the parish
no children .

Figure 6.12: train-jobtitles.txt: A short training file.

```
#!/bin/sh
# Shell script to train maxent models
# for OpenNLP-1.3.0 name finder
# G. Wilcock 21.11.2007
#
# Usage: ./opennlp-nametrainer.sh training.txt jobtitle.bin.gz

OPENNLP_HOME=~gwilcock/Tools/opennlp-1.3.0
export OPENNLP_HOME

CLASSPATH=.:\
$OPENNLP_HOME/lib/opennlp-tools-1.3.0.jar:\
$OPENNLP_HOME/lib/maxent-2.4.0.jar:\
$OPENNLP_HOME/lib/trove.jar
export CLASSPATH

java opennlp.tools.namefind.NameFinderME -encoding ASCII $*
```

Figure 6.13: `opennlp-nametrainer.sh`: A script to train new models.

clergyman with *clergyman* marked as a job title, the statistical model might recognize similar cases with a pattern like *Her ...ther was a ...man*. Other correct job titles would be *seaman* and *policewoman* in sentences like *Her brother was a seaman* and *Her mother was a policewoman*.

The disadvantage of using a statistical model is that false positives are found if they are similar to the given examples. In Figure 6.14, *woman* is marked as a job title in the sentence *Her mother was a woman ....* This is not surprising as *woman* ends in *...man*, which is a useful clue to recognizing other job titles like *clergyman* and *seaman*, and the pattern matches *Her ...ther was a ...man*.

6.4   COREFERENCE RESOLUTION

Coreference was discussed in Chapter 2, Section 2.7. Automatic coreference resolution is difficult, and is an on-going research topic. There are a number of reasons why it is difficult. It requires both linguistic knowledge and knowledge of the world, and these are already difficult areas when taken separately.

COREFERENCE ACROSS SENTENCE BOUNDARIES

One problem is that coreference occurs across sentence boundaries as well as within sentences. Figure 6.15 shows part of *Northanger Abbey* with coreference analysis by GATE. Chapter 5, Section 5.2 shows how to use the nominal and pronominal coreferencers. In the text in Figure 6.15, there are 14 occurrences of the pronoun *she* and 11 occurrences of the pronoun *her*, spread over 9 sentences. In every case these pronouns refer to the same person, Catherine Morland, with one exception. The exception is in the phrase *and Mrs. Morland, who did not insist on her daughters being accomplished...* where *her* refers to Mrs. Morland, not Catherine.

```
CHAPTER 1


No one who had ever seen <person>Catherine Morland</person> in her
  infancy would have supposed her born to be an heroine.
Her situation in <jobtitle>life</jobtitle>, the character of her
  father and mother, her own person and disposition, were all
  equally against her.
Her father was a <jobtitle>clergyman</jobtitle>, without being
  neglected, or poor, and a very respectable man, though his name
  was <person>Richard</person>--and he had never been handsome.
He had a considerable independence besides two good livings--and
  he was <jobtitle>not</jobtitle> in the least addicted to locking
  up his daughters.
Her mother was a <jobtitle>woman</jobtitle> of useful plain sense,
  with a good temper, and, what is more remarkable, with a good
  constitution.
```

Figure 6.14: Results of training with the short training file.

Human readers use knowledge of the world, and knowledge of the story, to understand the references. We know that Mrs. Morland is Catherine's mother, and *her daughters* refers to Mrs. Morland's daughters, not Catherine's. The previous sentence says *at eight years old she began*, so we know that Catherine is eight years old and does not yet have any daughters of her own.

GATE has successfully linked most of the 25 pronouns to Catherine Morland across multiple sentences, but has not recognized that Mrs. Morland and Catherine are different persons. The main error is in the sentence that mentions Catherine's sister Sally. In this sentence there are four occurrences of *her* or *she*, and GATE links them all to Sally. It is a good heuristic rule to link female pronouns to a female name mentioned in the same sentence, but in this case it is wrong. These four pronouns all refer to Catherine, who is not mentioned in that sentence.

Figure 6.16 shows part of the LingPipe coreference analysis for the same text from *Northanger Abbey*. Like GATE, LingPipe has successfully linked most of the pronouns to Catherine across multiple sentences, but has not recognized that Mrs. Morland and Catherine are different persons.

COREFERENCE AND SYNTACTIC RESTRICTIONS

Figure 6.17 shows part of the OpenNLP coreference analysis for the same text from *Northanger Abbey*. Chapter 3, Section 3.7 shows how to use OpenNLP coreference linker. As coreference resolution requires both linguistic knowledge and world knowledge, OpenNLP tries to use both. OpenNLP coreference uses linguistic information from OpenNLP syntactic parser, and uses information from WordNet as a substitute for knowledge of the world.

Like GATE, OpenNLP has successfully linked most of the pronouns *she* and *her* to Catherine Morland across multiple sentences. This can be seen in Figure 6.17 by the use of reference #36 for Catherine and the same reference #36 for the pronouns. Unlike GATE, OpenNLP has not treated Mrs.

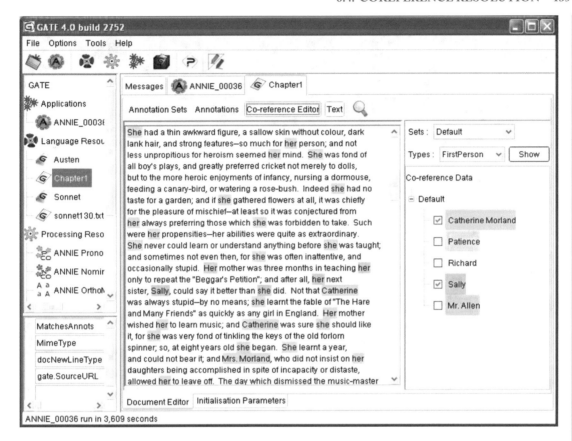

Figure 6.15: GATE Pronominal Coreference

Morland (reference #47) and Catherine (reference #36) as the same person. OpenNLP also does not equate Catherine's mother (reference #58) with Mrs. Morland (reference #47).

As well as knowledge of the world, human readers use knowledge of syntactic restrictions to understand the pronoun references, though this is normally not done consciously. In the sentence *Mrs. Morland, who did not insist ..., allowed her to leave off*, we understand that the person who was allowed to leave off was Catherine. This is partly world knowledge: we know that the person who began was Catherine, so we expect that the person who stops is the same person who began. In addition, there is a syntactic restriction: we know that the person who did the allowing is not the same person who did the leaving off, because that would require a reflexive pronoun *herself*. It would have to be *Mrs. Morland ...allowed herself to leave off*.

These syntactic restrictions on pronoun coreference are known as *binding theory* in linguistics. A detailed but clear analysis is given by (Sag et al. 2003). Despite using the syntactic information from the OpenNLP parser, OpenNLP coreference misses this syntactic restriction, and gives the non-reflexive pronoun *her* the same reference #47 as the subject *Mrs. Morland*.

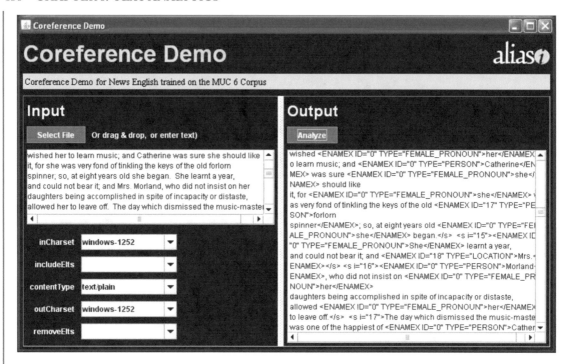

Figure 6.16: LingPipe coreference demo.

6.5   INFORMATION EXTRACTION

In this section we show how a commercial tool, IBM LanguageWare Resource Workbench (LRWB), can be used to create UIMA annotators for information extraction. The annotators can be deployed in UIMA applications using PEAR. As LRWB has its own user documentation, our examples do not give detailed instructions. See the *Getting Started Guide* (IBM 2008).

IMPORTING AND CUSTOMIZING DICTIONARIES WITH LRWB

LRWB uses language-specific dictionaries for lexical analysis (tokenization and tagging) and domain-specific dictionaries for gazetteer lookup (for named entity recognition). LRWB dictionaries are stored as databases, normally as embedded Apache Derby databases (http://db.apache.org/derby).

LRWB provides support for importing existing dictionaries, with conversion from XML or CSV (comma-separated values) formats. XML dictionaries are converted by LRWB using XSLT. LRWB provides an example XSLT stylesheet to be customized for the specific XML format. CSV dictionaries are converted automatically by LRWB. In CSV format, each entry is on a separate line with its fields separated by commas. Dictionaries in spreadsheets and databases can easily be exported in CSV format.

GATE gazetteer lists are simple lists with one entry per line, so they are in fact in CSV format (with no fields and no commas). They can therefore be imported directly into LRWB as CSV format dictionaries. Figure 6.18 shows an LRWB dictionary for job titles, which has been imported from the

```
(TOP (S (S (S (NP#58 (NML#36 (PRP$ Her)) (NN mother))
 (VP (VBD wished) (S (NP#36 (PRP her))
 (VP (TO to) (VP (VB learn) (NP (NN music)))))))) (: ;)
 (CC and) (S (NP#36 (NNP Catherine)) (VP (VBD was) (ADJP (JJ sure)
 (SBAR (S (NP#36 (PRP she))
 (VP (MD should) (VP (VB like) (NP (PRP it)) (, ,)
 (SBAR (IN for) (S (NP#36 (PRP she)) (VP (VBD was)
 (ADJP (RB very) (JJ fond) (PP (IN of) (S (VP (VBG tinkling)
 (NP (NP (DT the) (NNS keys)) (PP (IN of) (NP (DT the) (JJ old)
 (NN forlorn) (NN spinner)))))))))))))))))))) (: ;)
 (S (ADVP (RB so)) (, ,)
 (PP (IN at) (NP (CD eight) (NNS years))) (JJ old)
 (NP#36 (PRP she)) (VP (VBD began))) (. .)) )
(TOP (S (S (NP#36 (PRP She))
 (VP (VP (VBD learnt) (NP (DT a) (NN year))) (, ,) (CC and)
 (VP (MD could) (RB not) (VP (VB bear) (NP (PRP it)))))) (: ;)
 (CC and) (S (NP#47 (NP (NNP Mrs.) (NNP Morland)) (, ,)
 (SBAR (WHNP (WP who)) (S (VP (VBD did) (RB not) (VP (VB insist)
 (PP (IN on) (NP (NP (NML#36 (PRP$ her)) (NNS daughters))
 (VP (VBG being) (VP (VBN accomplished)
 (PP (IN in) (NP (NP (NN spite)) (PP (IN of)
 (NP (NML (NN incapacity)) (CC or) (NML (NN distaste))))))))))))))))))
 (, ,) (VP (VBD allowed) (S (NP#47 (PRP her))
 (VP (TO to) (VP (VB leave) (PRT (RP off)))))))) (. .)) )
```

Figure 6.17: OpenNLP coreference resolution in *Northanger Abbey*.

same GATE gazetteer list that we used in Section 6.2. The dictionary is being customized using the LRWB Eclipse interface. The entry for *father* is being removed.

PHRASE RULES
Once dictionaries have been created (or imported) to recognize relevant words, rules can be defined to combine them. In LRWB there are 3 kinds of rules: phrase rules, entity rules, and relationship rules.

A phrase rule is being defined in Figure 6.19. This rule combines a first name annotation and a last name annotation to make a person name annotation. The rules are easily created using the Create Rules interface shown in the figure. You specify which kind of rule you want to make (here, a phrase rule). You drop an extract from the text (here, *Catherine Morland*) into the Selection tab Input Text box and it is immediately parsed. You select from the parsed features exactly the ones that you want to be used in the rule. You specify the name of the new annotation (here, PersonName), and compile the rule. Note that this is much easier than defining JAPE rules in GATE.

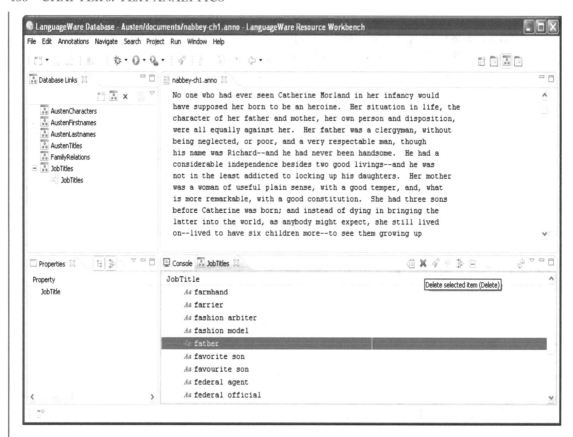

Figure 6.18: LRWB: Making a job titles dictionary.

In this example, only `AustenFirstnames` and `AustenLastnames` are selected. The specific token features are deselected. This makes the rule more general. For this rule it does not matter what string the tokens have, or what part of speech. All that matters is that there is an occurrence of `AustenFirstnames` followed by an occurrence of `AustenLastnames`.

ENTITY RULES
An entity rule is being defined in Figure 6.20. This rule takes a person name annotation and creates an entity annotation of type Person. The rule type for Entities is selected. The same extract from the text (*Catherine Morland*) has been dropped into the Selection tab and has been parsed. In the Annotation tab, the name of the new entity annotation is being specified as `Person`. This rule says that if something is a `PersonName` it is also a `Person` entity.

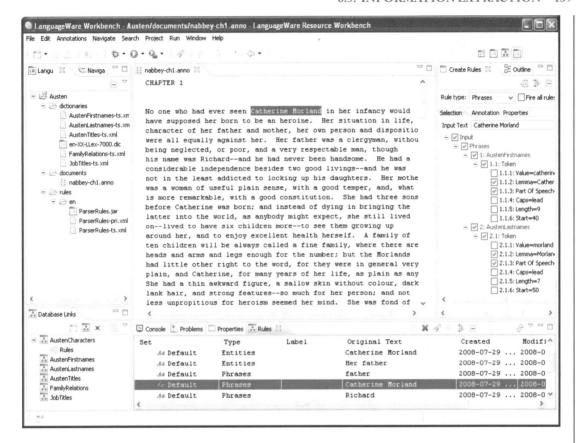

Figure 6.19: LRWB: Making a phrase rule for person names.

NAMED ENTITY RECOGNITION

It is easy to make a customized dictionary for family relations like *father* and *sister*. Then an entity rule can be created that recognizes phrases such as *her father* and *his sister*, and says that these are also Person entities.

With rules to recognize both named persons such as *Catherine Morland* and references to family members such as *her father*, it is possible to do named entity recognition for entities of type Person in *Northanger Abbey*. The persons identified in Chapter 1 are listed in Figure 6.21.

INFORMATION EXTRACTION AND RELATION EXTRACTION

The term *information extraction* is used in more than one way. Sometimes it simply means extracting any kind of information from texts, for example a list of job titles mentioned in *Northanger Abbey* (clergyman, music-master, …). In this sense it can be equivalent to named entity recognition. It is also used with a more restricted meaning, equivalent to *relation extraction*. Relation extraction requires not only identifying

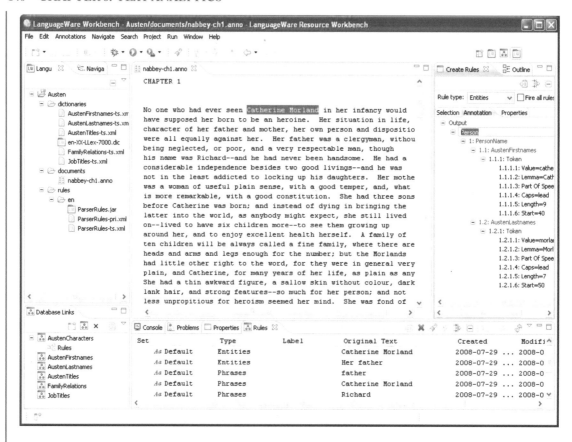

Figure 6.20: LRWB: Making an entity rule for Person entities.

significant entities but also identifying significant relationships between entities or significant properties of entities (Richard Morland is a clergyman, …).

In the MUC conferences, information extraction was also known as template filling, as the aim of extracting the information was to fill specific slots in predefined templates. The template might be *occupations*, and the slots might be *person* and *job*. The fillers might be *person: Richard Morland* and *job: clergyman*. These templates are typically stored as relations in a relational database. This is described in Section 6.6.

RELATIONSHIP RULES

In LRWB, relation extraction is done by relationship rules. They are created in a similar way to phrase rules and entity rules. Figure 6.22 shows a rule being created for occupations.

The rule type for Relationship is selected. The extract *Her father was a clergyman* from the text, that shows an example of the relationship, has been dropped into the Selection tab and has been parsed. This rule takes a `Person` and a `JobTitle`, and says that they are in an `Occupation` relationship.

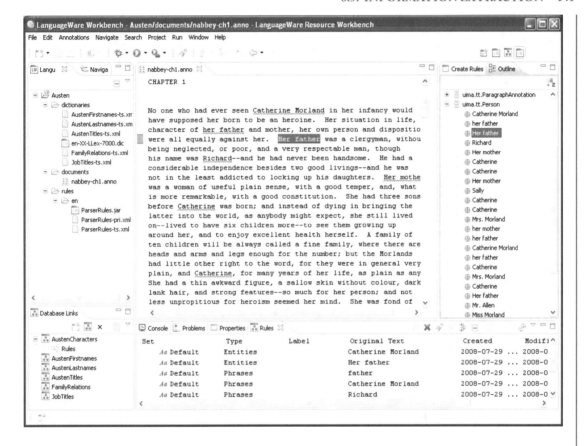

Figure 6.21: LRWB: Person entities in *Northanger Abbey* Chapter 1.

After the `Person`, the rule requires a token whose lemma is *be*. For this token the feature `Lemma=be` is selected, but the feature `Value=was` is deselected, so it will match any form of the verb *be* (such as *is, are, was, were, …*). Before the `JobTitle`, the rule requires a token whose part of speech is `Determiner`. For this token the feature `Lemma=a` is deselected, so it will match any determiner (such as *a, an, the, …*).

Relationship rules typically apply to entities, and the entities can be assigned to named slots in the relationship, as shown in Figure 6.23. The `Occupation` relationship has a `person` slot and a `job` slot. The `person` slot is filled from the `Person` entity and the `job` slot is filled from the `JobTitle` entity.

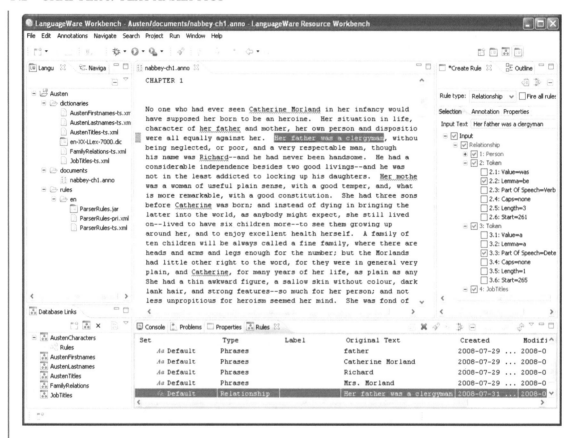

Figure 6.22: LRWB: Making a relationship rule for occupations.

6.6   TEXT MINING AND SEARCHING

DATABASES

The goal of information extraction is usually to store the extracted entities and relationships in a database. The tables in a relational database hold relations similar to the ones extracted from text by relation extraction.

The examples supplied with UIMA show how to write annotation results to a database. An example Java annotator recognizes `PersonTitle` entities, and an example CAS consumer called `ExamplePersonTitleDBWriterCasConsumer` writes `PersonTitle` instances to a database. The example uses Apache Derby (`http://db.apache.org/derby`), but any database can be used via JDBC.

The LingPipe website has a tutorial on *DB Mining* that shows how to do named entity extraction on text from a database, and store the results back into the database. The Java code examples use the LingPipe API.

The crucial point about storing relations in a database is that the information is *structured*. The information in the text is *unstructured*: there are different ways to express the same relation, different ways

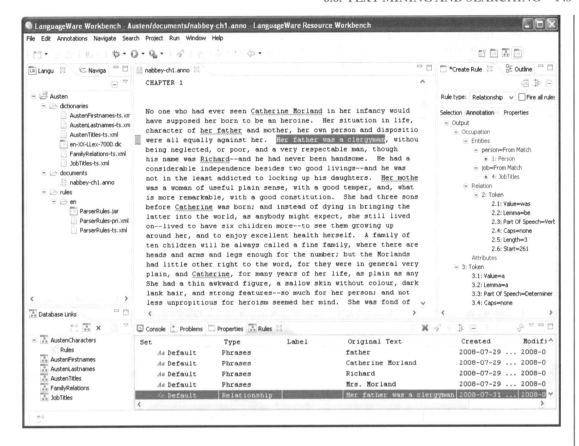

Figure 6.23: LRWB: Filling entity slots in a relationship rule.

to refer to the same entity, and ambiguity about which entity is being referred to. Natural language is notorious for its ambiguity and vagueness. By contrast, the database tables have exact names, the columns have exact names and data types, the entities that fill the rows and columns have unambiguous IDs. The conversion of unstructured information into structured information is the key task of text analytics.

DATA MINING AND TEXT MINING

Data mining usually refers to applications that apply statistical methods and machine learning techniques to structured information in databases, in order to discover new information by detecting patterns, trends and anomalies in the data. Data mining techniques are beyond the scope of this book.

Weka (http://www.cs.waikato.ac.nz/~ml/weka) is an open source data mining toolkit implemented in Java. A detailed introduction to data mining with practical examples using Weka is given by (Witten and Frank 2005).

Text mining, or *text data mining*, usually refers to applications that first perform information extraction from text, storing the results in a database, and then apply data mining techniques to the information in the databases. Of course, the information extracted from text may be combined with existing structured information that is already in the databases.

The main application domain for text mining so far has been biomedicine. The National Centre for Text Mining (NaCTeM) (`http://www.nactem.ac.uk`) in UK and the Jena University Language and Information Engineering (JULIE) Lab (`http://www.julielab.de`) in Germany both focus on this area.

SEARCH ENGINES

Search engines make it possible to search large collections of texts efficiently by constructing indexes. This requires some kind of linguistic processing, at least tokenization of the texts. Other processing may also be performed, depending on the kinds of search that are to be supported.

The familiar kind of searching is *keyword search*. The user inputs a natural language query, from which keywords are extracted. Alternatively, a keyword-only query is used. In either case, the index is searched using the query keywords, to find the documents that contain the keywords in their text.

It is common for indexes not to include "function words" such as determiners (*the, any*), prepositions (*of, at*), and conjunctions (*but, and*) because these words do not help when searching for "content words" such as *oxygen* or *malaria*. One way to exclude the function words would be to do part-of-speech tagging and then remove the determiners, prepositions and conjunctions. However, as these are closed-class words (the members of each category are fixed), it is faster to simply use a list containing all of them. These words that are to be excluded from the index are known as *stop words*.

Apache Lucene (`http://lucene.apache.org`) is an open source Java library for indexing and searching, which is very efficient and widely used for keyword searching. A good introduction is (Gospodnetić and Hatcher 2004). Lucene can also be used in combination with text analytics tools. Examples of using Lucene with GATE and LingPipe are given by (Konchady 2008).

SEMANTIC SEARCH

Semantic search uses some kind of *semantic index* as well as a normal keyword index. The semantic index is constructed by doing named entity recognition on the texts in addition to tokenization. The named entity recognizer annotates the entities with their type, such as `Person`, `Location`, or `Organization`. These annotations are indexed by the semantic index.

When the user inputs a query, named entity recognition is used to extract semantic types from the query, in addition to normal keyword extraction. In cases of ambiguity, some kind of clarification dialogue may also be used to confirm the semantic types. The semantic index can be used to improve the search in two ways. It can restrict the number of normal keyword matches by eliminating those which are the wrong semantic type. It can also be used to find semantic matches where the query keyword does not occur in the text at all, but the semantic types show sufficient relevance to return the match.

As Lucene and UIMA are both Apache projects, it is expected that good integration of UIMA annotations and Lucene indexing will be developed in the near future. Meanwhile, IBM has made available a semantic search package that was developed when UIMA was an IBM system, which uses IBM's Juru search library, not Lucene. It can be downloaded from `http://www.alphaworks.ibm.com/tech/uima`. A good overview of UIMA and semantic search is given by (Ferrucci 2006).

6.7   NEW DIRECTIONS

An important issue for the future direction of text analytics is whether UIMA will be widely adopted as a standard. UIMA has been welcomed and actively supported by academic research teams, but it appears that commercial text analytics companies prefer to keep to their own ways of doing things.

ONTOLOGIES

In Section 6.6, we said that one use for information extraction was to populate databases. An increasingly important variation on this is to populate ontologies. The ontologies provide a classification system, and the members of each class are found by *instance extraction* from texts.

A more advanced approach uses machine learning to construct the ontology classification itself from analysis of texts. These topics are beyond the scope of this book. GATE provides support for machine learning and for working with ontologies. Other open source Java tools include the Protégé ontology editor (`http://protege.stanford.edu`) and the Jena ontology programming framework (`http://jena.sourceforge.net`).

The UIMA architecture is based on typed feature structures, which depend on the definition of an appropriate type system. A type system is itself a kind of ontology. The relationship between UIMA type systems and OWL ontologies is a current research topic.

TEXT ANALYTICS WEB SERVICES

Calais (`http://www.opencalais.com`) is a commercial text analytics web service owned by Clearforest, a Thomson Reuters company. Gnosis is a web browser plugin that uses the Calais web service to perform named entity recognition for the web page you are viewing.

Figure 6.24 shows named entity recognition results for the start of the HTML version of *Northanger Abbey* at the Gutenberg Project website. Calais correctly classifies *Catherine Morland*, *Catherine* and *Mrs. Morland* as persons and identifies *cricket* as a sports game. Human readers understand that *Mrs. Morland* is *Catherine*'s mother, but Calais classifies them as the same person. As we saw in Section 6.4, getting this right is a challenge for coreference resolution.

Calais and Gnosis are not open source, but contributors to Apache UIMA have developed an open source UIMA wrapper for Calais. It is available from the UIMA Sandbox (`http://incubator.apache.org/uima/sandbox.html`).

6.8   FURTHER READING

- Message Understanding Conferences: See (Chinchor 1998).

- CoNLL conferences: See `http://ifarm.nl/signll/conll/`.

- Text Analytics Summits: See (Grimes 2008).

- Precision and recall: See (Manning and Schütze 1999) Section 8.1.

- Syntactic restrictions on pronoun coreference: See (Sag et al. 2003).

- IBM LanguageWare Resource Workbench: See (IBM 2008).

Figure 6.24: Calais text analytics web service.

Bibliography

Ahn, D., E. T. K. Sang, and G. Wilcock (Eds.). 2006. *Multi-Dimensional Markup in Natural Language Processing: Proceedings of the 5th Workshop on NLP and XML (NLPXML-2006)*, Trento. Association for Computational Linguistics.

Boguraev, B., N. Ide, A. Meyers, S. Nariyama, M. Stede, J. Wiebe, and G. Wilcock (Eds.). 2007. *The LAW: Proceedings of the Linguistic Annotation Workshop*, Prague. Association for Computational Linguistics.

Burke, E. M. 2001. *Java and XSLT*. O'Reilly.

Chase, N. 2005. Create a UIMA application using Eclipse.
http://www-128.ibm.com/developerworks/edu/x-dw-xml-i.html.

Chinchor, N. 1998. Overview of MUC-7/MET-2.
http://www.muc.saic.com/proceedings/muc_7_proceedings/overview.html.

Cunningham, H., D. Maynard, K. Bontcheva, V. Tablan, M. Dimitrov, M. Dowman, N. Aswani, I. Roberts, Y. Li, and A. Funk. 2009. *Developing Language Processing Components with GATE Version 5.0 (a User Guide)*.
http://gate.ac.uk/.

Cunningham, H., D. Maynard, K. Bontcheva, and V. Tablan. 2002. GATE: A framework and graphical development environment for robust NLP tools and applications. In *40th Anniversary Meeting of the Association for Computational Linguistics*, Philadelphia.

Ferrucci, D. 2006. UIMA and Semantic Search: Introductory Overview.
http://www.ibm.com/research/uima.

Ferrucci, D., and A. Lally. 2004. Building an example application with the Unstructured Information Management Architecture. *IBM Systems Journal* 43(3):455–475.

Finkel, J. R., T. Grenager, and C. Manning. 2005. Incorporating non-local information into information extraction systems by Gibbs sampling. In *43rd Annual Meeting of the Association for Computational Linguistics*, 363–370. DOI: 10.3115/1219840.1219885

Gospodnetić, O., and E. Hatcher. 2004. *Lucene in Action*. Manning Publications.

Götz, T., and O. Suhre. 2004. Design and implementation of the UIMA Common Analysis System. *IBM Systems Journal* 43(3):476–489.

Grimes, S. 2008. Text technologies in the mainstream: Text analytics solutions, applications and trends.
http://altaplana.com.

Hahn, U. (Ed.). 2008. *Towards Enhanced Interoperability for Large HLT Systems: UIMA for NLP*, Marrakech.

Hahn, U., E. Buyko, R. Landefeld, M. Mühlhausen, M. Poprat, K. Tomanek, and J. Wermter. 2008. An Overview of JCoRe, the JULIE Lab UIMA Component Repository. In *(Hahn 2008)*.

IBM. 2008. LanguageWare Resource Workbench Getting Started Guide Version 7.0. `http://www.alphaworks.ibm.com/tech/lrw/`.

Ide, N., P. Bonhomme, and L. Romary. 2000. XCES: An XML-based encoding standard for linguistic corpora. In *Proceedings of the Second International Language Resources and Evaluation Conference*, Paris.

Jurafsky, D., and J. Martin. 2008. *Speech and Language Processing: An Introduction to Natural Language Processing, Computational Linguistics and Speech Recognition. Second Edition.* Prentice Hall.

Klein, D., and C. Manning. 2003a. Accurate unlexicalized parsing. In *41st Annual Meeting of the Association for Computational Linguistics*, 423–430. DOI: 10.3115/1075096.1075150

Klein, D., and C. Manning. 2003b. Fast exact inference with a factored model for natural language parsing. In *Advances in Neural Information Processing Systems 15 (NIPS 2002)*, 3–10, Cambridge, MA. MIT Press.

Konchady, M. 2008. *Building Search Applications: Lucene, Lingipe and Gate.* Mustru Publishing.

Le Page, W., and P. Wellens. 2003. jEdit as an Advanced XML Editor. `http://www.adrem.ua.ac.be/~wellenslepage/jedit_as_axe/`.

Manning, C., and H. Schütze. 1999. *Foundations of Statistical Natural Language Processing.* MIT Press.

Marcus, M. P., M. A. Marcinkiewicz, and B. Santorini. 1993. Building a large annotated corpus of English: the Penn Treebank. *Computational Linguistics* 19(2):313–330.

Miltsakaki, E., R. Prasad, A. Joshi, and B. Webber. 2004. The Penn Discourse Treebank. In *Proceedings of the Language Resources and Evaluation Conference*, Lisbon.

Mitchell, T. 1997. *Machine Learning.* McGraw Hill.

Morton, T., and J. LaCivita. 2003. Wordfreak: An open tool for linguistic annotation. In *Proceedings of HLT-NAACL 2003, Demonstrations*, 17–18, Edmonton. DOI: 10.3115/1073427.1073436

Palmer, M., D. Gildea, and P. Kingsbury. 2005. The Proposition Bank: An annotated corpus of semantic roles. *Computational Linguistics* 31.1:71–106. DOI: 10.1162/0891201053630264

Ratnaparkhi, A. 1996. A maximum entropy model for part-of-speech tagging. In *Proceedings of the Conference on Empirical Methods in Natural Language Processing*, 133–142, University of Pennsylvania.

Ratnaparkhi, A. 1997. A simple introduction to maximum entropy models for natural language processing. Technical report, Institute for Research in Cognitive Science, University of Pennsylvania.

Reynar, J. C., and A. Ratnaparkhi. 1997. A maximum entropy approach to identifying sentence boundaries. In *Proceedings of the 5th Applied Natural Language Conference (ANLP97)*, 16–19, Washington, DC. DOI: 10.3115/974557.974561

Sag, I., T. Wasow, and E. Bender. 2003. *Syntactic Theory: A Formal Introduction*. Stanford: CSLI Publications.

Santorini, B. 1990. Part-of-speech tagging guidelines for the Penn Treebank Project.
http://repository.upenn.edu/cis_reports/570/.

Tidwell, D. 2000. Transforming XML Documents.
http://www.ibm.com/developerworks/edu/x-dw-transformxml-i.html.

Tidwell, D. 2001. *XSLT: Mastering XML Transformations*. O'Reilly.

Tidwell, D. 2002. Introduction to XML.
http://www.ibm.com/developerworks/edu/x-dw-xmlintro-i.html.

Tidwell, D. 2004. XML Programming in Java Technology.
http://www.ibm.com/developerworks/edu/x-dw-xml-i.html.

Toutanova, K., D. Klein, C. Manning, and Y. Singer. 2003. Feature-rich part-of-speech tagging with a cyclic dependency network. In *Proceedings of HLT-NAACL 2003*, 252–259, Edmonton, Alberta. DOI: 10.3115/1073445.1073478

Toutanova, K., and C. Manning. 2000. Enriching the knowledge sources used in a maximum entropy part-of-speech tagger. In *Proceedings of the Joint SIGDAT Conference on Empirical Methods in Natural Language Processing and Very Large Corpora (EMNLP/VLC-2000)*, 63–70, Hong Kong. DOI: 10.3115/1117794.1117802

Webster, J., N. Ide, and A. C. Fang (Eds.). 2008. *Proceedings of the First International Conference on Global Interoperability for Language Resources*, Hong Kong.

Witten, I. H., and E. Frank. 2005. *Data Mining: Practical Machine Learning Tools and Techniques*. Morgan Kaufmann.

Printed in the United States
by Baker & Taylor Publisher Services